Antler:

THE

SELECTED

POEMS

Antler:

THE
SELECTED
POEMS

SOFT SKULL PRESS
2000

Antler: The Selected Poems
© 2000 by Antler
Introduction © 2000 by Jeff Poniewaz
ISBN:1-887128-40-9

Front Cover Photograph: Spencer Tunick's "Scopes" Series
Frontispiece Photograph of Antler in 1977: Stanley Ryan Jones
Author Page Photograph: Steve Miles
Back Cover Photograph of Antler: Allen Ginsberg
Design: David Janik

PRINTED IN CANADA

Soft Skull Press
100 Suffolk St.
New York, NY 10002
www.softskull.com

TABLE OF CONTENTS

from *Ever-Expanding Wilderness*

INTRODUCTION

Books of Selected Poems don't usually come out after a poet has published only two books. Thus far, not counting five chapbooks and several unpublished book manuscripts, Antler has published just two books.

Completed in 1975, his *Last Words* did not appear until Ballantine brought it out in 1986. Of the five sections into which that edition was divided, the first three sections—subtitled "Last Words," "Factory" and "First Drink from a Stream"—comprised the original 1975 manuscript. For the 1986 Ballantine *Last Words*, Antler added two sections of poems that could have been published as a separate book if the original three-section *Last Words* had been published earlier: "Reworking Work" and "Catching the Sunrise."

It was surprising that this unique new poet encountered publication delays, considering he was one of the younger poets Allen Ginsberg most liked and recommended, who had won strong favorable response from both Ginsberg and Ferlinghetti as early as 1971. City Lights did publish in December 1980, as a book to itself in its "Pocket Poets Series" (#38), the long poem in thirteen sections titled "Factory" that comprised the middle third of the *Last Words* manuscript. So Antler's first book published, *Factory* in 1980, was actually the middle third of a larger book that ideally would have come out in 1976 but came out in 1986 instead.

Antler's bestfriend since we were 19 in 1966, I'm the person who sent his poems to Ferlinghetti for the first time in early '71, which drew a letter of response inviting us to have tea with him when we'd be in San Francisco that summer. The very same week in August '71 Ferlinghetti sang us "Dark Ages Over Now" in his City Lights office, I twisted bashful Antler's arm to give a manila envelope full of his poems to Allen Ginsberg for the first time after a reading Allen gave with Philip Whalen in North Beach upon Allen's return to the USA from India. It was a dream come true that his revered Beat father figures, both Ginsberg and Ferlinghetti, responded enthusiastically to the pleasant surprise of this exciting new poet who appeared out of the blue from the heart of the Heartland.

Therefore Antler didn't expect he'd have any problem getting a book in print when the time came. He trusted to "the serene brotherhood of philosophs" Whitman urged poets to be: being kind and generous to one another and beaming equanimity and magnanimity to all humanity as in Walt's "Salut au Monde," Allen's "Who Be Kind To" and Ferlinghetti's "To Poets with Love."

Perhaps due to sunspots combined with a strange hex of events, the poetry scene weirded out a bit between 1975 and 1980, just when Antler came forward from his early years of solitude poetry apprenticeship with an amazing book called *Last Words*. He came to discover Allen's advocacy of his poetry was a two-edged sword and a coat of many colors. Kindhearted junior "love-nut" Antler found himself an innocent bystander caught in the crossfire of "poetry wars."

Acclaim from a wide spectrum of poets, environmentalists and factory workers that greeted the 1980 City Lights edition of *Factory* provided consolation for publication tribulations up till that time. As a result of the City Lights *Factory* and new poems he published in periodicals and anthologies, Antler won the 1985 Whitman Prize awarded to the author "whose contribution best reveals the continuing presence of Walt Whitman in American poetry."

Lots of factories have closed down since Antler proclaimed "the extinction of factories" circa 1970, though new "Factory" poems are no doubt being written by Third World poets even now, working on the same machines exported overseas. Besides factory work, the poem tackles our ongoing dysfunctional economy and work "ethic" in general and the environmental impact of the escalating world population of workaholic mega-consumers. So Ginsberg's initial assessment of the poem still rings true: "Here's a prophecy beyond Factory to new Eden in aeonic mind-space."

In 1984 Allen published in *CoEvolution Quarterly* (put out by the *Whole Earth Catalog* people) a spread of funny rejection letters rejecting famous books—a parody he wrote in response to Antler's continuing difficulties finding a publisher for his *Last Words*. A rejection letter from Jason Epstein of Random House turning down Antler had inspired those parody letters. When a copy of that spread came to Epstein's attention, it led to *Last Words'* publication at long last by Random House's Ballantine subsidiary in 1986.

In 1990 when Antler was at his peak of giving readings around the country, both the City Lights *Factory* and the Ballantine *Last Words* went simultaneously out of print. They sold well for poetry books in late 20th Century America. They weren't remaindered; the publishers just didn't reprint them. City Lights may have thought that since the Ballantine *Last Words* included "Factory," it was unnecessary for City Lights to keep a separate edition of "Factory" in print. And then Ballantine simply decided to stop publishing poetry books altogether and publish only the types of books that make more money.

In 1991 a millionaire publisher from St. Louis offered Antler $12,000 to reissue *Last Words* and publish his nextbook manuscript, but as part of the deal he wanted Antler to sign over his copyrights and original manuscripts. When Antler phoned Allen for advice, Allen told him he should never sign away copyrights and should save his original manuscripts as "insurance for his old-age." So Antler turned down the millionaire's twelve thousand.

Across the 1990s, several publishers came close to accepting Antler's nextbook manuscript *Ever-Expanding Wilderness*, but wound up deciding that though they liked Antler's work it was a tad too wild for them or "a bit too much of a stretch from our current list of authors." Worry about jeopardizing grants during the Jesse Helms era no doubt influenced some of those decisions. Antler never expected when he embarked on a course that so wholeheartedly responded to Whitman's and Ginsberg's exhortations to candor, that as a result he'd have so much trouble finding a publisher so many years after Walt and Allen flung wide the door for all-out open-hearted honesty.

The good news is he never stopped writing, never let himself get that bummed out, didn't vanish mysteriously into the wilderness he loves like Lew Welch vanished into the wilderness he loved. When his books went out of print, new poems by him kept coming forth in periodicals and anthologies. And now I take joy in the re-appearance in bookform at long last of some of Antler's very best poems from *Last Words*, including "Factory" complete, plus a panoramic preview of the poems in his thus far unpublished nextbook manuscript, *Ever-Expanding Wilderness*.

It's good to know for historical context that the poems in the 1986 Ballantine edition of *Last Words* were written from 1966 to 1983, including additional poems written while the original 1966-75 manuscript was seeking a publisher, and that the poems in *Ever-Expanding Wilderness* span 1983-1999. And it's important to know that *Factory* was written by a young poet 24 years of age circa 1970 while working in a factory during Nixon's presidency and the Vietnam War, though it unfortunately wasn't published until the month after Reagan knocked Carter out of the White House.

The moral of this story for poets getting discouraged by publication delays may be to harken back to a little 1855 Brooklyn printshop where an unknown poet named Walt Whitman paid to have his own slim volume of verse printed and set some of the print himself. Despite Emerson's enthusiastic blurb on the second printing of that self-published book, Whitman still had to self-publish several of the subsequent editions of his *Leaves of Grass* over the years.

This new and selected volume was commissioned by Allen Ginsberg not long before he died. He connected Antler to the young rebel publishing outfit that seemed to him a sign of hope in his Lower East Side Manhattan neighborhood, which for Allen represented the generation to which the torch would have to pass. Therefore this Selected—drawn from only two books, it's true, but two *big* books (*Last Words* with "Factory" in it and the thus far unpublished *Ever-Expanding Wilderness*), each containing as many poems as two or three usual-size poetry books, and spanning 1966 to 1999.

Antler's acknowledgment list at the end of this volume is huge, far longer than for any poetry book I've ever seen. It testifies to his determination to keep his poetry in circulation—in periodicals and anthologies at least—during a time when it was unavailable in book form: to keep his work alive in all the bioregions of America, to convey the gift he was given to give. It shows his sense of responsibility to honorably fulfill his poet vocation against whatever odds, and also shows he honors the little magazine / small press tradition. Many of the periodicals are "major," but many more are the heroic "mags" of small circulation that uphold a healthy spirit of democracy to temper the tendency toward a literati hierarchy.

Another moral of Antler's story is to keep writing, no matter what: never forget that the writing of the poem is the most important thing, beyond all vexations of publishing and literary scene. "Apart from the pulling and hauling stands what I am," wrote Whitman, and that's where Antler has taken his stand, too.

Antler is the Savage in Brave New World who *didn't* kill himself. May his liberating, large-hearted poems never go out of print again, so they can help open minds enough to figure out a way to that "new Eden": to halt and heal the eradication of the Wild, inner as well as outer, and nurture its return as we enter a century in which the previous two centuries' assaults on Nature threaten vast catastrophe.

—Jeff Poniewaz
Milwaukee, Wisconsin
July 2000

from **LAST WORDS**

Trying to Remember What I Learned

The old classroom is alone in me
Trying to remember what I learned.
Desktops wrinkled with words.
Under the seats, fingerprints of gum.
Pen on the floor, tip finely chewed.
Listen for the echo of milkteeth.
Not even the janitor
With his broom and red sawdust
Stands here in the middle of night.
Ropes of shades are tied in delicate nooses.
The clock ticks in a circle
Of ages I once was.
This building's a stone
Names wander in and out of,
Laughing when they find their name
The same as the name in a book.
The globe is dark. I used to spin it
And let my finger find where I was going.
The blackboard is clean,
No streaks where moist sponges passed over.
Erasers rest in their troughs,
Thick with white chalk dust.
In one eraser more knowledge
Than hundreds of books?
The chalk rubs off on my fingers
Minute fossilized creatures
That lived millions of years ago.
The fire escape has never been used.
I had to learn all these words.

Rexroth as He Appeared to Exist

March 24, 1968 9:00 P.M.

It was as if he were slowly falling asleep,
Sitting in that chair, while everyone at the party
      asked him questions.
Suddenly I wondered if someday I'd become a bard
And if, as they asked me questions,
         I'd tilt back my head and for a minute or so
         pretend to doze, eyes peering under lids,
And I wondered if then, in that future crowd,
There'd be anyone like me who once
      couldn't think of any questions to ask,
And couldn't help but think: how soon
      he will be dead
And that's how he'll look in the coffin,
      head back like that
      with Halley's Comet hair.
Years from now when I hear the news of his death
I'll remember that night and this poem,
Shivering a little as I did then,
Surprising myself
      with the thought of salmon
      shooting up the rapids of his brain,
What he was—near as a grosbeak, far as Orion,
      the sound of mice moving delicately
      in the walls of his flesh.

Metaphor

Seeing a boy stare in through the glass,
The adult magazine store where I'm standing,
I know he's aching for pictures of skin
That can make a metaphor of his hand,
Thinking of times his house is suddenly empty
And rushing her familiar flesh from hiding
He can fill his bed with nakedness and dream
She touches him softly as a mirror.
And I think of Hypatia,
Lecturer in philosophy at the Alexandrian Museum,
Who, though loved by many, remained a virgin.
Once, when a student confessed his total love,
She, lifting her dress to her waist, said:
"What you love is this,
And nothing beautiful."
And here stands this boy
Who must close his eyes to see
A girl more real, more naked
Than pictures.

For Those Who No Longer Go Ahhh...

Not watching the fireworks
I thought how much more beautiful
Were the faces illuminated—
Some thinking for the first time
How like orgasm the explosions,
A thought now old to me,
Yet for them how much meaning,
I knew, I remembered.

Out of our lives forever
Hundreds of fireworks faces.
Where they are going
Is to the sigh and dissolution
After the flashing flower,
After the falling petals,
Silence looking upward
Hoping what's next is more beautiful.

Last Words

As this girl lay asleep on the beach
An ant crawled up her nose and laid its eggs
And when they hatched and ate into her brain
She clawed away her face and died screaming.
Or that deep-sea diver whose pressurized suit burst
Who was squeezed a liquid pulp of flesh
Up the air hose onto the deck,
A long strand of human spaghetti.
Or that man on a Japanese train killed by the severed leg
Of a suicide who jumped from a passing train,
A hundred miles an hour through his window.
Or Li Po launching himself like a paper boat toward the moon.
Or Aeschylus strolling along the shore
When an eagle, looking for a stone to crack a turtle's shell,
Spotted his pate gleaming in the sun.
Or that Pompeii boy immortalized in lava.
Or the unearthed coffin, the lid scratched and bloody inside.
Or abandoned by his family, the old Eskimo circled by wolves.
Or Superman no longer faster than a speeding bullet through his head.
Or Santa's helicopter crashing in a shopping center of expectant children.
Or six children trampled to death in Cairo by a mob
Rushing to a church where the Virgin had just appeared.
These deaths speak for themselves. They don't need last words.
As for me, I'm not looking into the sky for falling flowerpots.
Yet any second sights of a rifle may fix upon my brain.
Fourteen humans walked alive that day a perfect stranger
By the name of Whitman up in a tower of higher learning
Shot them down one by one. Just like that. Dead.
I think of that old man stoned by three children
        who jeered him out of his house.
If someone told me that's how I'd die in fifty years
I wouldn't believe it. Did anyone tell the old man?

How will I die? Cleaning a gun with my eyes?
Walking into a mirror? Driving into a tree to avoid a porcupine,
        my learner's permit in my pocket?
I know the old philosophies. Yes, I've already died in a way.
My boyhood and all that. Showers of fingernails and hair.
The constant sloughing off of the cells of my body.
The death of all the semen that has left me.
My turds, moving to their own bewildered death.
Maybe it'll be like that first night in San Francisco
Waking up to go to the bathroom in Milwaukee,
And getting out of my old bed I walk into a new wall.

Maybe it'll be coming up or going down stairs in the dark
Thinking there's one more step when there isn't
Or not one more step when there is.
Will I choke on a bone, or be swallowed by a whale?
Or a death brimming with allusions—
Tugging a book from the tightly packed shelf
        I pull my whole bookcase over on me.
Or slow death: torture, cancer, leprosy, senility,
Or exotic: voodooed, cannibalized, human-sacrificed,
        devoured by man-eating plant.
Which is worse, being eaten alive or starving to death?
Dying crying for help or begging for mercy?
Yawning as the bomb drops in my mouth,
Sneezing in the avalanche zone,
Done in by hiccups that can't be stopped,
Or like in Stekel, that man who hid under the outhouse seat
And disemboweled his wife from beneath with a butcher knife.
        I look before sitting.
Or seeing my ultimate vision of absolute beauty
I scream as in horror comics—"AAARRRGGGHHH!!!"
Will I die laughing? Be struck by lightning?
        Will I never know what hit me?

Maybe the sky will fall on me.
Maybe the ground'll just open up under me.
Maybe a gang of boys'll pour gasoline over me and light me.
        Or will it be a case of spontaneous combustion?
Will I be mistaken for a deer during deer season?
Or like Tita Piaz who climbed 9000 feet of sheer rock 300 times
        with his son strapped to his back, only to die in a fall
        down his steps?

And when am I going to die?   I'd like to know.
I don't want to get there when the show's half over.
I don't want to fall asleep. I'll have to poke myself.
I don't want to miss my death the way I missed my birth.
I sit here and plan my last words. I'm going to be prepared.
As in murder mysteries where the victim lies dying
And the hero holds him and says—"Who did it?"
In the same way they'll gather round me and ask—
        "What does this poem mean?"
        or "Do you really think *that* is beautiful?"
And then, like the murdered victim, I'll mumble far away
Feverishly trying to think of something profound and rising in pitch gasp
"It was It was It was It was..."
Then slumping back I die.
What will I say? Shall I make fart sounds with my lips?

Should I tell where the treasure's hidden?
Should I utter *Wanbli Galeshka wana ni he o who e*?
      My bestfriend's name?
Or make make-believe deathrattles better than birdlovers
      warble songs of their favorite birds?
Or should I join the chorus of thousands who shriek "AAAIIIEEE!!!"
      or the thousands who simply go "O"
      or "Ugh" or "Oof" or "Whoops"
Or should I press finger to lips in the sign of silence?
Not content with ruling the world, Nero, wanting to be its
      supreme actor and musician, ordered full houses and
      awarded himself all the prizes, and while he sang
      no one could leave, though many pretended to die
      in order to be carried out as corpses. Shall I say
      as he did when forced to commit suicide—
      "What a great artist the world is losing!"
Or like Rabelais—"Bring down the curtain the farce is finished,"
      and later as the priests surrounded him,
      he, with a straight face, sighed—
      "I go to seek a great perhaps."
Or like the Comtesse de Vercelles, according to Rousseau—
      "In the agonies of death she broke wind loudly. 'Good!'
      she said, 'A woman who can fart is not yet dead.'"
Or like Saint Boniface as boiling lead was poured down his throat—
      "I thank thee Lord Jesus, Son of the Living God!"
Or Saint Lawrence, broiled on a gridiron—"This side is done now,
      turn me over."
Or Emily Dickinson—"I must go in, the fog is rising."
Or Beddoes—"I ought to have been among other things
      a good poet."
Or Lindsay, full of lysol—"They tried to get me . . .
      I got them first."
Or Socrates—"Crito, I owe a cock to Asclepius,
      will you remember to pay the debt?"
Or Chopin—"Swear to make them cut me open
      so I won't be buried alive."
Or Scriabin, his face engulfed in gangrene—
      "Suffering is necessary."
Or Marie Antoinette, having stepped on the executioner's foot—
      "I beg your pardon."
Or Huey Long—"I wonder why he shot me?"
Or Millard Fillmore—"The nourishment is palatable."
Or P.T. Barnum—"How were the receipts today
      in Madison Square Garden?"
Or Carl Panzarm, slayer of 23 persons—"I wish the whole human race
      had one neck and I had my hands around it."
Or Jean Barre, 19, guillotined for mutilating a crucifix—

"I never thought they'd put a gentleman to death
        for committing such a trifle."
Or da Vinci—"I have offended God and man
        because my work wasn't good enough."
Or Vanzetti—"I am innocent."
Zeno, founder of the Stoic school, striking the ground with one fist—
        "I come, I come, why do you call for me?"
W. Palmer, stepping off the gallows—"Are you sure it's safe?"
Metchnikoff the bacteriologist—"Look in my intestines carefully
        for I think there is something there now."
John Wilkes Booth—"Tell my mother I died for my country."
Dylan Thomas—"I've had 18 straight whiskies. I think that's
        the record."
Dutch Schultz—"French Canadian bean soup!"
Byron—"I want to go to sleep now."
Joyce—"Does nobody understand?"

Must I be the scribe of each word I speak,
        never knowing if it will be my last?
Or should someone else be my full-time scribe
        (in case deathfits keep me from writing them down)
Always ready to put ear to my lips
        in case it should be a whisper?
"Rosebud." "More weight." "More light."
"Now it is come." "Now I die." "So this is death?"
"Thank you." "Farewell!" "Hurrah!" "Boo!"
        "Can this last long?" "It is finished."
Or like H.G. Wells—"I'm alright. Go away."
Or like Sam Goldwyn—"I never thought I'd live to see the day."
Or like John Wolcott when asked if anything could be done for him—
        "Bring back my youth."

I tell myself what my last words will be,
Hoping I don't get stage fright.
Hoping I don't get laryngitis.
Hoping someone will hear them.
Hoping I'm not interrupted.
Hoping I don't forget what they are.
From now on everything I say and write
Are my last words.

Applause

Striking the palms of hands together, quick smart blows,
       producing abrupt sharp sounds,
       expresses their satisfaction.
After the performance, they do this.
It is called clapping. I sit and observe,
       that my actions will not be improper.
Am I allowed to do this? Softly at first, I begin,
       scared the man next to me may growl—
       "Quiet! Don't you know this is for *us* to do?
       Children should be seen not heard. Grow up!"

Am I a grown up? I've made up my mind.
But how should I hold my hands?
Up to my breast, or down by my genitals?
Cupped and weak, or flat and firm?
Elbows flush with my sides, or flaring?
Should one hand be still (which one?) and be slapped by the other?
Or should I take wide strokes with both as if trying to take off,
       or pull invisible taffy?
What's the rhythm, rapid or slow?
Do I pat daintily with nose in the air?
Or hard like pounding a nail in?
I'm not used to hitting myself.

Ladies flowing in minks (little stuffed heads
       with black plastic eyes staring from breasts)
       tap their programs on purses.
They've squinted at them throughout the performance,
       rustling the pages, fanning their faces.
       As they leave they forget them.

How many came to hear the music?
How many secretly hoped the performer would make a mistake
       or forget the piece halfway through?
How many nodded off digesting their dinners,
       or peered sideways searching for someone attractive?
Where are those who disappeared during intermission?

I think of cabbages and tomatoes hurled on stages of yore.
I think of orgious ovations lasting three hours.
Why at the end of a symphony doesn't the audience
       carry the players off on their shoulders
       like fans pouring onto the field after a victory?
Hugo's *Hernani*, on opening night

the audience burned down the theater
and tried lynching the actors.
On "Queen for a Day" mothers broke down competing at misery,
while the applause-o-meter leapt to crown
the champion of disasters.

Are they afraid not to clap?
They don't need idiot cards.
After the most passionate music they clap loudest.
They know how to break the spell.
Is the sound of their clapping more beautiful than the music?
Why don't they clap through the entire performance?
After all, who's really performing?
What does the virtuoso think when at the last note—cough, cough
and then the avalanche of praise?
Does he listen to the textures of thousands of fingers?
Does he go into the audience asking for autographs?
Does he lob rotten eggs at the box seats?
Does he clap for himself?
He's seen the seals at the zoo.
If the audience really appreciates beauty why don't they scream
for hours, clapping till their hands get so hot they melt off
and they clap faster and faster with their feet and
they drop off and they clap their limbs, teeth, gums,
intestines and genitals till all that's left is a huge arena
of smoking dismembered bodies?

I'm waiting for the time when no one claps.
Paralyzed in silent epiphany. Hands frozen in prayer.
Who claps for lightning?
Who claps for the bowel movement?
After apocalyptic orgasm who claps?
Who claps at a great man's death?
How many are virtuosos of their lives?
People were applauding when Lincoln was shot.
When Jesus was crucified who applauded?
Who stood and demanded an encore?
What kind of ovation did he get?
Blake saw his brother's soul rise through the ceiling
to heaven, clapping.
Coffin lids clap only once.
If we must clap, why can't it be in soundless slow-motion
like a butterfly drying its wings?
I clap with my eyes.
My heart claps with one hand.

When I think of my death do I imagine my favorite symphony

rising to climax and I, maestro at the finale,
     collapsing with romantic gesture,
     audience filing out silent with heads bowed?
Beethoven at the premiere of his Ninth, stone deaf,
     conducting the last time in his life—
     when it was over, he, being several measures off,
     kept waving his arms during the deafening roar.

Audience and performer are gone now, and I'm still sitting.
Clapping. I've learned how. I'll always clap last
     so I add to the total performance.
My art is small, yet heard after all.
Do you think I stay home nights to practice my clapping?
Or am I designing concert halls with pillories for hands?
Am I just one of the audience who couldn't go home
     without finding what he lost:
     a wallet, a scarf, a key, the program
     on which I jotted notes for this poem?

Once at a reading I deliberately clapped after a lousy poem.
Soon the whole room was earthquaking claps:
Clap. CLAP. CLAP. CLAP!CLAP!CLAP!
     CLAP!!CLAP!!CLAP!!CLAP!!
Do you think I like applause after this poem or any poem?
Do you think I love the silence after my voice has stopped?
Yet I've heard the refusal of praise is only the wish
     to be praised twice.
Each clap stings like the challenge to a duel.
The clock's hands clap as I grow old.
The typewriter claps as I write this.
Can clapping ever be the same?
After reading this will I hear only breathing?
After writing this will I sit here and clap loud and long?

The Bewilderment of Laughter

A boy and girl walk past you laughing,
And because they're laughing and you're not,
And because you don't know why they're laughing,
  it's as if they're laughing at you,
Even if they're not,
Even if they're laughing so hard
  they don't even notice you as they pass,
And so walking alone becomes walking lonely,
For no matter how many friends you have
A boy and girl will walk past you laughing
  sometime when you're alone,
And because what's loneliest in you will hear them,
The sound of their laughter will haunt you
  long after they're gone.

So when old men slip and laugh as they fall
  you ask them to be your teachers,
To teach you where Christ laughs in the gospels—
A laugh that makes others laugh,
  a funny laugh, a contagious laugh,
A laugh impossible to hold back,
  a wild laugh, a consoling laugh,
A laugh more profound than prayer or parable,
  a believable laugh,
A laugh that unfolds like a head of lettuce,
  a fresh green laugh,
A laugh that makes heaven without laughing unthinkable,
A laugh that curls lips back not to bare fangs to scare rivals,
A laugh that spreads in ripples till it's lapping round the world,
A laugh only had it been recorded
  slaughter would never have the word laughter in it
  and no one would ever abominate
  the merriment of worms.

But nowhere in scripture does it say "Christ laughed."
Nowhere does he split a gut!
Nowhere does he somersault and cartwheel hooray!
Nowhere does he hug himself laughing himself hoarse!
Nowhere does he jump-up-and-down-laugh-his-ass-off-whoopee!
Nowhere does he spend 40 days and nights in omnipotent conniptions!
Nowhere does he give immortality to fun or the bliss of glee
  or teach a Lord's Prayer full of wisecracks!
And where is he giddy or silly?
And where is he drunken with laughter?

And where does he fracture his funnybone?
And where does he wear jester shoes with curled toes and little bells?
O point out the chapter and verse of his slapstick slaphappy laughter!
Where does he tell how the man without a jaw laughs?
Where does he say the reason we bury corpses
            is because they get funny?
Why didn't he make making fart sounds under armpits his disciples?
Why isn't giggling while hiding playing hide'n'seek in the twilight
            a beatitude?
Why isn't baptism epilepsies of laughter?
Wouldn't everything be different if just once the Son of God
            had bent over and cracked a smile?
Was Christ only pulling our leg about eternal damnation?
            (Heaven really only for atheists and heathens?)
When the nails were pounded in
            did no one see the twinkle in his eye?
Did no one but me hear the jokes he told from the cross?
Don't you think he got a kick out of sticking his finger
            through the holes in his hands?
Don't you think he ever chuckled to himself as he walked alone?

Our way of laughing grows older as we do:
For some of us it dies before our funeral—
Suddenly we hear ourselves laughing
            like someone who will never be an actor,
And we realize years ago we didn't like people
            who laughed like that.
So we listen to recordings never made
            of laughter bubbling from our mouths
            five, ten, fifteen, twenty, twenty-five birthdays old,
Remembering uncontrollable laughter possessing us
            till it hurt so much we laughed even harder,
            wetting our pants from laughing so hard,
            laughing until we cried....
And so we start repeating the word death over and over,
Death with the word eat in it that will eat us,
Death that's not sorry we tamed our laugh
            so we can turn it on and off like a lightswitch,
Death that sheds no tears we busted our laughingfit buckingbronco,
Death that does not care if we think death is no laughing matter,
Death that does not say death is the punchline,
Death that does not say death has the last laugh,
Death that's never been Christ's flunky or yes-man,
Death that doesn't give a damn if Christ died laughing or cursing,
Death that doesn't consider Christ getting a boner on the cross a blasphemy,
Death that doesn't have to swear on a stack of Bibles to tell the Truth,
Death that doesn't give a hoot if we believe no matter how we live

if we can make God laugh we are saved,
Death we want to believe will touch us like our mother,
        like the mother who consoles her child
        when other children point and laugh,
Death with its skull that never stops grinning
        the grin that never stops touching
        our face from the inside,
And babies may cry when they're born
        but their skulls have been grinning long before
        and don't need a university to learn how,
And how a blind man feels when everyone's laughing
        and he can't see what's so funny,
And how this all brings us back to the boy and the girl,
How they walk toward us and past us laughing
        or from behind us and past us laughing
And walking lonely not laughing we wish we could join them,
        wish we could fill our mouths with those jubilees.

II

All I've done is fill my mouth with words.
I've composed haikus to monkeyshines and odes to shenanigans.
I've authored the epic of tee-heeing on tip-toe.
I've dissertationed the definitive text of ticklishness.
I've sent humoresque smokesignals from the ancient peaks.
I am the scholar of winks and the archeologist of guffaws.
I've traced the word for laugh in every language back to the sun.
The giggling of Neanderthal children in caves during the sacred ritual
        still reaches my ears.
I hear laughter of rolling down hills and leaping off sand dunes.
I hear laughter of fathers running with sons
        laughing piggyback on their shoulders.
I hear laughter of mothers holding daughters by hands
        and going in a circle so fast
        the little girls fly around in the air.
Yet where is the deep spontaneous laugh I haven't laughed in years?
        My primal laugh, my inexhaustible laugh?
        The laugh in which all of me laughs, not just my mouth?
O how many fatted calves would I kill
        if my laugh that was lost was found?
Will I never again feel the thrill
        breaking up in church so the whole pew shakes
        with wrestled-back gags of laughter?
Will all the times I imitated laughter of morons and opera singers
        never return the way it made all my friends laugh?
And the laughter of my sixth grade class

when the teacher didn't see my raised hand
and I ran up to tell her I felt sick
and before I could say a word
vomited on her dress
to become laughingstock of the school for weeks,
Can't I look back on it now and laugh?
I feel like a stone face that's frowned for 5000 years!
Must I wait for all the faces I made in the mirror to become my face
before delighting in a single cackle?

If there is one laugh worth all the laughs you have left,
take it now,
And after that thigh-slapping, floor-rolling binge
You won't have to ask— "How long have deformities and deathcamps
been God's court jester?"
You'll know why children draw the sun with a smiling face.
You'll understand how maniacs can laugh for hours.
You'll know what lies behind the laughter of peekaboo
and ring-around-the-rosy,
And the laughter of girls in junior high showerrooms,
And the laughter of boys pretending to get dirty jokes,
And the toothless laughter of nursing homes,
The laugh of those finding out they have one month to live,
The laugh of the waterskier rising in bubbles
as he rises to surface into the returning propeller,
The laugh of dolls you pull the string from their backs and they laugh,
The laugh of the rapist or strangler who has cornered his victim,
The laughter of men who make a living poisoning the Earth
and don't feel guilty,
The laughter of crowds at public tortures and executions,
the laughter of the guillotined head,
And the hermit who hasn't seen a human in thirty years
listening to the echo of his laugh across the valley,
And the laughter of siamese twins joined at the mouth,
The laughter of the man the Sioux buried up to his head
smeared with honey near an anthill,
Laughter of ants, laughter of anteaters,
Laughter of monkeys and laughing hyenas,
Laughter of aspen and weeping willow,
Laughter of lizards and lampreys and clams,
Laughter of whales and amoebas,
Laughter of volcanoes and earthquakes,
Laughter of exploding stars,
Laughter of earthlings oggling Earth from the moon,
Laughter of the crescent moon's smile,
Laughter of other planets,
The laugh of those who scorn poetry,

The laugh of those deaf since birth,
Obnoxious laugh of those who laugh too loud and long,
Nervous laugh of the inexperienced teacher,
Derisive laugh of the perverted embalmer,
And those who laugh in the face of death,
And those who laugh bad breath in your face,
And those who laugh at their own bad jokes,
And those who laugh behind laughing masks,
And those who laugh through their nose,
And those who laugh while they cry inside,
And those who dimple at the dimpling of buttocks,
And those who double up at the bullfrog's croak,
And those whose job is turning people into pretzels of laughter,
And the man in stitches who splits into stitches—
All the gales of laughter, all the tons of laughs,
        all the laughs in the world
        you will understand.
For as long as you stand under the waterfall of all the laughs of your life
        in an instant
How can you be sad? How can you be lonely knowing a trillion years
        is only a second in Eternity?
And looking through a telescope large as our galaxy
        with an eye big as the sun
Why be unhappy because you can see no more of Infinity
        than an infinitesimal crumb?

Someday you could find yourself when the bird sings in the forest
Listening like the bird to its own overflowing song,
About to discover you can sing without words
        or the lilt of some tune,
That tossing your head back it would rise
        and you'd let it, your laugh,
The way you laughed as a child, your tears,
        the way they loved coming from joy,
Your laughter, your tears, together—
        HO spelled backwards OH,
        HA spelled backwards AH—
And the bird listening as you are
        to both of your songs.

Factory

The machines waited for me.
Waited for me to be born and grow young,
For the totempoles of my personality to be carved,
    and the slow pyramid of days
To rise around me, to be robbed and forgotten,
They waited where I would come to be,
    a point on Earth,
The green machines of the factory,
    the noise of the miraculous machines of the factory,
Waited for me to laugh so many times,
    to fall asleep and rise awake so many times,
    to see as a child all the people I did not want to be,
And for suicide to long for me as the years ran into the mirror
    disguising itself as I grew old
    in eyes that grew old
As multitudes worked on machines I would work on,
    worked, ceased to exist, and died,
For me they waited, patiently, the machines,
    all the time in the world,
As requiems waited for my ears
    they waited,
As naked magazines waited for my eyes
    they waited,
As I waited for soft machines like mine
    time zones away from me, unknown to me,
    face, flesh, all the ways of saying goodbye,
While all my possibilities, like hand over hand on a bat
    to see who bats first, end up choking the air—
While all my lives leap into lifeboats
    shrieking—"You can't afford to kill time
    while time is killing you!"
Before I said *Only the religion whose command before all others*
    is Thou Shalt Not Work shall I hosanna,
Before I said *Not only underground are the minds of men*
    eaten by maggots,
Before I said *I would rather be dead*
    than sweat at the work of zombies,
The machines waited.

Now the factory imagines I am there,
The clock keeps watching me while it works
    to see how much time it has left.

How much does it get paid? Are coffins the safes
        where it keeps its cash?
I see my shadow working on the shadow of a machine.
Everywhere I look I am surrounded by giant machines—
Machines that breathe me till I become stale
        and new windows of meat must be opened.
Each year of my name they ran, day and night,
Each time I kissed, each time I learned a new word,
        or name of a color, or how to spell boy,
Night, day, without stopping, in the same place running,
Running as I learned how to walk, talk, read, count, tell time
        and every time I ever ran alone
        pretending to be a wild black stallion,
They ran as I thought never (my eyes in the clouds)
        would my future corpse need to be buried
        premature in slavery of exchange to comtemplate
        the leisure vacations of photosynthesis and limnology
        and the retirement of tombstone inscriptions
        into veils that veronica the Earth,
They ran, and I never heard them,
        never stopped to hear them coming,
All the times walking to school and back,
All the times playing sick to stay home and have fun,
All the summers of my summer vacations
I never once thought I'd live to sacrifice my dwindling fleshbloom
        packaging the finishing touches on America's decay
For money to earn me so I can write in the future
        about what I am now, then am no longer,
Shortening the lifespan of planet for 6 cents a minute
        so I can elegize the lifespan of beauty and my life,
So I can say before my parents ever met
        machines were blaring the same hysterical noise,
So I can say they were waiting for me
        every mouthful of food I swallowed,
So I can say they were waiting for me
        every time paper eyes of paper nakedness
        watched my hands perform the ritual of dreams,
So I can say each second so many die so many are born,
        like rapid snapping of fingers, snap, snap,
        snap you live, snap you die, snap you live and die again!
Each day of my life *is my life!*

So, winding my watch before work
        with the galaxies of my fingerprints—
        each twist of my lifeline a dungeon of ticks—
I wondered was it for this
        my hide'n'seek Huckleberryhood?

And pondered how each day goes to its grave single file
        without the corpse of what I might have been,
Yet the hour hand is so slow
        no one will ever see it move.

Each of the great works never written
By those who work in factories so they can write words,
        what they say will be great words,
Does not care, does not wait to be written—
At the end of a day's work he who left his mind
        eight hours at his writing desk for the repugnance
        of metal on metal, noise on noise,
Sits down with his pen as if he had already written
        the great words of his dreams.
His feet feel like nursing homes for wheelchairs,
His ears an inferno of crickets,
And he says—"I feel like the grave of someone I loved"
And dreams of being hired to hammock-drowse
        outside where workers work
        to comtemplate the utopias of sleep
Or to conduct tours of the plant reciting by heart
        the godliest glossolalias of divine frenzy.
Each day, those reaching the cliff of their last words
        waterfall into the gorges of night, wondering
How much do corpses get paid for working underground?
How much should they receive for urging their eyes to become
        the eyes on butterfly wings, peacock tails, and potatoes?
How much to package their innards into the innards of trees
        and leaves that creep down shirtfronts of children hiding in them?
How much to coax their hearts into the eight hearts
        of the hermaphroditic nightcrawler or into the pink stars
        that are the noses of moles?
What Union do corpses join? How do they feel, more segregated
        than old people, when we keep them from humans that live—
        as if their bodies weren't the bodies we loved
        and called by the names we loved them by—
        and cut the dandelions from their faces?

Perhaps I have never left the factory.
Perhaps I'm made to dream the 16 hours my identity flees.
It's the drug in the water that does it, remarkable.
To think I'll work here forever thinking I go home and return
        and do all sorts of things in between,
        like writing this poem—
Of course I'm not writing this poem!
I'm on the machine now packaging endless ends of aluminum
        for the tops and bottoms of cans.

Our foreman laughed— "You'll wake up in the middle of the night
        as if you're working. It's so easy
        you can do it in your sleep."
And I know that in one day owning this place
I'd make more than if my life worked my lifetime here.
In my lifetime I'd make more than all the workers combined.
Then I could envy those who make a million a second—
To them the prostitutes must be most beautiful
        and pornography a religion that is never disbelieved.
To those, this memo, dashed during breaks in slavery
        whose chains regenerate faster than tails of salamanders
        or penis's reengorgement.
To my soul wondering if I have a body or not: Huck, Huck,
        look down at your funeral from lofts of the barn o' blue,
Look down at me dreaming my deathbed in factory,
        machines gone berserk, drowning in a sea of lids,
Dying where no one could hear my last whisper
        for industries of scholars to unhieroglyph—
Where the noise is so loud that if I screamed louder than I can
        no one would hear me, not even myself,
Where the bathroom stalls are scratched with the multiplication
        of men's lives in money, the most begging graffiti,
Where it is not I who wrote this tomb, but a machine,
        and the earplugs, and the timeclock
Waiting so many times to pick up the card that tells me my name,
Where metal cries louder than human yearning to return underearth,
And the first shift can't wait to go home,
And the second shift can't wait to go home,
And the third shift can't wait for the millions
        of alarmclocks to begin ringing
As I struggle with iron in my face,
Hooked fish played back and forth to work
        by unseen fisherman on unseen shore,
Day after day my intestines unwinding around me
Until I am a mountain of waste
From whose depths all that is left of me,
        a penis and a mouth,
Dreams of reaching the peak of all I contained,
Dreams of jerking that fisherman from the earth
        and dragging him to the pearls
        in the jaws of the giant clams of the sky....

II

"All you have to do is stand here
        and package lids as they come from the press
        checking for defects every so often.
Shove enough lids in the bag like this,
Stand the filled bag on end like this,
Fold over the top like this,
Pull enough tape off
        and tape it like this,
Then stack 'em like this on the skid."

How many watching me watch the woman
        teach me my job
Remembered *their* first day on the job,
Remembered wondering what the woman felt
        teaching them in a minute
        the work she'd done all her life,
Showing them so fast all they needed to know?
How many could still remember who they were in search of a living—
Name, address, telephone, age, sex, race,
Single, married, children, parents, what they do or why they died,
Health record, police record, military record, social security #,
        how far in school, everywhere worked, why quit or fired,
        everything written here is true, signature, interview,
        the long wait, the call "you're hired"—
Could still see themselves led through the factory
        to the spot they would work on,
        strange then and now so familiar?

This is the hall big as a football field.
Here are the 24 presses chewing can lids
        from hand-fed sheets of aluminum.
Here are the 10 minsters chomping poptops
        nonstop into lids scooped into their jaws.
Machines large as locomotives,
        louder than loudest rockgroup explosions,
Screeching so loud you go deaf without earplugs,
        where the only way to speak is to gesture,
Or bending to your ear as if I were telling a secret
        the yell from my cupped hands less than a whisper.

Now the film of myself each day on the job begins.
I see myself enter the factory, led to the spot I will work on.
I see myself adjusting the earplugs to stopper the deluge of sound.
I see the woman who showed me the job
        she'd done her whole life in a minute

Let me take over, and the minute she left how I fumbled,
        how the lids gushed all over the floor
And when the foreman rushed over and I hollered—
        "Something's wrong! It's too fast!
        No one can work at this speed!"
How he stared and the stares of the others
        who couldn't hear what I said but could tell.
And I gulped, This "Beat the Clock" stunt
        must be performed *eight hours*
        before the lunatic buzzer itself
        becomes consolation prize.

Yet sooner than I thought, I mastered the rhythms,
        turned myself into a flywheel dervish,
And can't deny being thrilled by the breakthrough
        from clumsy to graceful—
Though old-timers scowled as if it took years
        to learn all the fine points.
But long after my pride in doing such a good job
        turned into days crossed off the calendar
        each night before pulling out the alarm
                I woke to push in,
        up, eat, go, work, eat, work, back, eat, sleep,
All the days I would work stared
        ahead of me the line of machines,
        behind me the line of machines,
Each with a worker working as I work,
        doing the same job that I do,
Working within sight of the wall clock
        whose second hand is still moving.

                            III

Thus as the foreman watched me from the corner of his eye
        as I watched him from the corner of mine
        pretending to be doing my best
                as if I didn't know I was under inspection,
I relished the words I would write
        intoned in this factory where no one could hear them,
        swallowed in the shrill-greased ecstasy of machines
                as I led processions of naked acolytes
        sopranoing Athenian epitaphs, candles in their hands.

To write this poem, to bring the word "beautiful" into Factory
You must never forget when the lids first come from the press
        they are hot, they are almost slippery.

You must never forget since each tube holds 350 lids
        and each crate holds 20 tubes and each day I fill 40 crates
From my work alone 280,000 lids each day—
        huge aluminum worm wriggling one mile long
        into the cadaver of America.
You must never forget 14 million cans each day
        from a single factory!
5,110,000,000 cans each year from a single factory!
More throwaway cans each year than human beings on planet!
Every high, every heartbeat of your life
        the machines have been running.
Every time you heard a pianissimo
        the earsplitting machines have been running.
You've already spent more time working here
        than making love,
More time working here than lying on hills
        looking at the sky.
Each of your favorite books you must pilgrimage here
        to absorb and exude wisdom,
To think of those who worked here before you
        and those who will work here after you.
You must say to yourself—"If I don't work here
        this poem won't be able to write me."
And asked—"What's that smell?" you must remember
        on your clothes, on your skin, in your lungs
        and when the breeze is just right through your bedroom window
                the smell of the factory.
You must brainstorm machines and workers are like poets and readers:
        the poets eat sheets of steel and press them into words
                that are the ends of containers,
The reader stands in one place shifting from foot to foot,
        crating and crating,
Searching for defects so the noisemaker can be shut down
        and while white-coated mechanics scurry to fix it
        like doctors around a sick president, he can take a break,
        get a drink, take a crap, unwrap some butterscotch to suck on,
                glimpse a glimpse of second-shift sunset,
                watch the guard lower the flag.

To birth this womb, to do for Continental Can Company
        what Walt Whitman did for America,
You must celebrate machine-shop rendezvous!
You must loafe observing a disc of aluminum!
You must sing the security of treadmills
        remembering where you are today
                you were yesterday
                you will be tomorrow.

So, after suicide invites you through the naked mirror
        and poetry dares you to dive headfirst into the sky,
After memorizing the discovery of fire, tools, speech,
        agriculture, industry,
And all the inventors, inventions and dates
        of the last 10,000 years you got a 100 on in History,
And after the ceaseless history of human war
        reads the eyes in your face,
Faced with the obituary of man,
Caught in the deathrattle of the world,
        from the deathblows of pollution,
        from the deathknells of overpopulation,
        from factories which are the deathbeds of Nature
                and the seedbeds of bombs,
After contemplating the graveyard of elegies,
        the immortality of maggots
        and the immolation of the sun,
Then, Antler, or whatever your name is,
Enjoy returning prodigal to your machine
        to forget the view from the skyscrapers of money,
        to forget the hosts of human starvations
                belly-bloated or brainwashed in Mammon,
        to forget the sign over the entrance to Auschwitz
                WORK MAKES MAN FREE,
        to forget that working here you accomplice
                the murder of Earth,
        to forget the birds that sing eight hours a day
                daydreaming the salaries of worms,
        to forget how old you must be
                to be rich and young before you die,
        to forget your mother waking you
                from this nightmare
                is only a dream—
So nothing called life can torment you with undertakings
        and your only responsibility toward mankind
                is to check for defects in the ends of cans.

IV

All I have to do is stand here
        and do the same thing all day.
But the job requiring five steps repeated over and over
        eight hours every day
                is not monotonous.
Only the body and mind finding such work monotonous
        is monotonous.

Those who gripe work is boring
        gripe they are boring.

Yet if I work hours and the clock says
        only five minutes has gone by,
If the last hour working seems longer
        than the seven before it,
Won't my last day on the job seem longer
        than all the months that preceded it?
Could I have been here more in one day
        than someone who's put in ten years?
Or has he learned how to punch in and out
        fast as a punching bag?
Don't we both know the way
        to the prong of our alarm in the dark?
How long could I work without looking up at the clock?
How long before I was watching its hands
        more than watching my own package lids?

It's not so terrible that every second dies
        or that whatever I am every second dies
        or that what we call death
                is death only of the final second,
But it is terrible (not like movies that lead us
        down corridors to doors springing slimy buffooneries)—
Terrible as having to eat meat killed in factories is terrible,
        as having to wear clothes made in factories is terrible,
        as having to live in homes built by strangers
                and exist among millions of strangers
        and be born and buried by strangers is terrible,
Too terrible for "terrible" to have any meaning—
        that every second dies
                whoever I could possibly be.

V

Standing in one place all day,
Howl of machines too loud for anything but solitude,
Rhythm of work-movements long ago involuntary as breathing,
As seconds become minutes become hours become days
        become weeks become months
What goes through your brain?
What carries you away?
What soars?

Whatever thought me while I slaved, remember me now!

Conceive me again! Inspire! Absorb! Engross me again!
Come, power of this very spot—
        overwhelm me again!
Fast-motion film of evolution
        on this spot where I work—
Start from the start and leave nothing out!
Provoke me as you provoked me then!
        Confront me as you confronted me then!
Begin to consider me, everything that happened,
        is happening, will happen on this specific intersection
                of latitude and longitude!
        I dare you to run wild in me again!
Show me every ocean, mountain, forest, glacier
        that once actually was where the machine is now!
Show me the pageant of every creature
        born or died on this point on Earth,
        that sexed here or ate here or played here
                or slept here for here was its home!
Show me this factory grown old, abandoned in ruins!
Show me what stands where it stood
        every sunrise the next billion years!
Let me piece together civilizations that don't yet exist
        from their imagined remains!
How long before who's exactly beneath me on the other side of globe
        tires of thinking me?
How long before what every living thing's doing as I work
        no longer fascinates me?
Everywhere I could be and everything I could be doing right now—
        Stagger me with instantaneous travelogues!
Seductive documentaries of every point on Earth—
        Tantalize me again!
O Reveille my Reveries to Revelry again!

Which volume from the limitless libraries of my imagination
        should I curl up with first?
The Complete Poetry of Australopithecus?
The Complete Poetry of the Shelley of 3000?
My autobiography before birth? My autobiography after death?
Maybe you'd like to bury your nose in "Puberty of Smell"?
Would you rather browse through "Charon's Coin Collection"
        or "Learning to Breathe"?
Would you rather check out "Putting Mountains Inside Me"
        or "Turning Myself Into Earth"?
Or why not let the wind turn to the page that begins—
        "Even the most ethereal vision of the mystic
                is knowledge much as an amoeba
        might be said to know a man."

Or why not the snapshot album of faces
        of everyone committing suicide this second?

Every second I work millionaires younger than me
        are fulfilling my wildest desires.
Do other workers love their genitals
        as much as I love mine?
The middle-aged women know how much sex
        the young guys need to think and have.
Old-timers pin nudes above their last stand,
        play tag with lids whizzed at each other,
        the foreman pretends not to notice.
Wistful penises, wistful vaginas
        hark back to their boyhoods and girlhoods
        growing up oblivious to lifetime in factory.
Ah, daydreams of fucking! It's true
        after six hours you've exhausted the repertoire
                but there's nothing like having a boner
        when there's no way to touch it and it won't go away,
And clearer than ever before the old man I become
        pictures my puberty passion—
Just how my penis began making love to me,
        how girls' nipples swooned for my mouth,
How the mirror put its lips against mine
        and kissed me deep with its boyish tongue!

How many boys are assembling plastic models of dinosaurs
        in Wauwatosa this second?
How many boys are pretending their hands are dogfighting biplanes
        in Wauwatosa this second?
How many boys are riding bikes with feet on the handlebars singing
        in Wauwatosa this second?
How many boys are playing "Engulfed Cathedral" on the piano
        in Wauwatosa this second?
How many boys are reading *Martin Eden* in Wauwatosa
        falling in love with poetry this second?
How many boys are jacking off in the Universe this second?

What good does it do to say one second
        is to a human lifetime what a human lifetime
                is to the age of the Milky Way?
What good does it do to say there are as many galaxies
        in the visible universe
                as stars in the Milky Way?
What good does it do to say each of us is a planet
        or that there are millions of planets
                with life in outerspace?

The workers look forward to lunch
    or fucking when they get home.
Long nights of TV look forward to them.
Weekends of movies and bars look forward to them.
Cheering in football stadiums and buying things in stores
    and 50 weeks imagining a 2-week vacation,
        all are waiting for them.
Does the baby inside the pregnant woman working ahead of me
    dream of a knock on the door and a check for a million?
When she smokes by the vending machine on her break
    and it's not as if she's staring off into space
    but as if space were staring far off into her eyes,
        can the unborn tell the dead from the living?
Are its ears already dumbfounded by stupor?
Does it already treasure Te Deums of tedium?
What good does it do to say each of us is a universe
    when we're bored with immortality already?

Poetry keeps telling me I'm an obstetrician on 24 hour call
    to deliver the voice of God from my mouth.
Beethoven had a chamberpot installed in his piano bench—
    there wasn't time to leave the keys.
I can't hear the Moonlight without seeing him write it,
    his britches around his ankles.
How long would it take to hear all he wrote
    if I listened eight hours a day?
How long must I dream of squeezing as fast and thick and warm
    for hysters to truck away for consumers to guzzle
    the hops of my nostalgia?
How much do beetles deserve for rolling dung into balls
    to cradle and suckle their young?
Do ants carrying away my lips get overtime?
What kind of raise do corpses get?
What kind of promotion?
How long before the canteen of melodies you can hum
    runs dry?
Or all the poems learned by heart as you toiled,
    typed on small cards—"Poets to Come,"
    "The World Is Too Much With Us," "Man With the Hoe,"
    "Ozymandias," "Mezzo Cammin," "Divina Commedia #1,"
    "There Was a Boy," "In Paths Untrodden," "Gic to Har,"
    "Ode to West Wind, Melancholy, Grecian Urn, Nightingale,"
    "Shine, Perishing Republic," "Futility," "The Broken Oar,"
    "Hay for the Horses," "A Blessing," "To a Stranger,"
    "Strange Meeting," "The Waking," "In a Dark Time,"
    "The End, The Beginning," "Vulture,"

"Lines Writ by One in the Tower
        Being Young and Condemned to Die". . .
How long before they get sick of chanting you aloud?

One June afternoon on my break
I walked to the plant entrance and found
A storm, incredible rain, lightning and thunder,
        sky suddenly so dark the street lights came on,
And noticed, on the ground by the open door,
Hundreds of cigaret butts left by those
        who stood, at some time, on the same spot,
Facing the guardhouse, the parking lot, the lawn after that
        to the street, the other factories this side and across,
                the busy freeway beyond,
And realized no one working could hear the thunder,
        no one working could see the rain.

Why aren't the workers memorizing geologic time charts on the job,
        dates of eras and forms of extinction on their fingertips?
Are they bored with the full-length re-runs of their past?
Aren't they happy with a free lifetime supply of dreams?
What ten desert islands have they picked to take with them
        to Megapolis?
I can still hear them saying to each other—
        "It seems I just get out of work and I have to go back."
        or "I look upon it like it's just one big joke."
        or "At least it's not a concentration camp."
Have none of them heard the fog asking to be let in
        to engulf each minion in cool mist?
Does no one remember how they first pronounced
        the Book of Job?
Is no one intoxicated with their philosophy
        of getting high?
Is this death's way of greeting me
        at the beginning of a great career?

VI

Millions of humans enter factories at dawn.
How many have their arms raised to the sun?
How many want to be late? How many demand to be fired?
Faces leaving as I arrive, faces arriving as I leave—
        It's too easy to say they are zombies.
(Am I not also singing—"I have to go and die some more
        so that my corpse can live"?)
Even a zombie can think all it makes in its life

31

is to some no more than a penny.
Even the daydreams of zombies are full
        of all that cocks and cunts can do.
What does it prove that I can write
        De mortuis nil nisi bonum
        on the bags of lids bound for the minsters?

I know I can die without having read any great,
        without having tried sex everyone I found,
        without climbing the highest or sailing the largest alone,
        and without scrawling the great worms of my dreams—
I know life does not care how much we make of it.
Nor does death care, unconcerned with our last words
        or the way we dispose of corpse and grief
        or whether these assumptions are correct
                or whether anyone says—
        "I will worship the spirit of the naked worm
                until death believes in me."
And I know the sun doesn't care if we make our own clothes
        and build our own homes from skins
        of animals we hunt and kill for our food.

When the bombsquad failed to locate the bomb
Someone called up to say would blow up the plant
And the foreman was ordered to order everyone back in,
As the workers returned to drudgery's smithereens
        while kids on summer vacation whizzed by on bicycles
How could I help wishing I'd been the disguised handkerchief
        phoning the bosom to go off?
Ironic, thought I, if this anarchrist explode under me
        as I slaved for the tycoon's cigar!
Suddenly my fingers were once more setting fire
        to miniature models of military reality—
        plastic construction kits of death glued lonely nights
        watching horror films on TV—battleships named after states
        filled with matchheads and firecrackers
        demolished with joy.
Yet what does this prove? Even these inklings can swarm
        in the corpse-brains of zombies.

                        VII

Sometimes I wish there were a log cabin
In the most deafening part of the factory
        where I could hermitage
        listening to the wind over the chimney,

And every so often as I wrote
        peer out through the shade-edge
        to see the workers working so hard,
And wonder if they ever figured out
        how many lids they touch in a day,
Or if they ever open a can and wonder
        if they've already touched it
Or what lips touched what lids
        they held in their hands,
Or what they'd think of this poem.
Or if they ever considered the can—
How in 1810 the first can was made,
How the first skilled workers could make
        only one by hand an hour,
How today's machines make 1000 a minute,
How America uses 115 million cans each day,
200 billion cans used in the world each year,
Each year enough metal used making cans
        to pave a ten-foot-wide highway to the moon!

Soon no one will be left to lift old cans like skulls
        to contemplate who quaffed the ravished brides of quietness.
The can-littered streams will remain
        long after America has to be memorized
        by the children of other planets.
Who will remember Continental Can Company
        was the foremost aluminum polluter on Earth?
The five billion bacteria in a teaspoon of soil?
The million earthworms per acre?
What bug? What fish? What frog? What snake? What bird?
        What baluchitherium or pteranodon?
                What paleolithic man?
How can I apologize to primeval shorelines cluttered with beercans?
Should I say I needed the money?
Should I say my body is the bible of flies?
Should I say each lid weighs more than an orgasm?
Should I say what if machineroar were rainsong or cricketsong?
Should I say I'm a spy behind enemy lines,
        what top secret will I escape with?
Should I say here's a free pass
        to the antique beercan collector's convention?
Must the beercan on the mountainside
        always be part of the view?

VIII

Now I understand why one Sunday night
I found myself the only one working in factory,
Given what is not given to every longing for loneliness:
    eight hours of pure underworld,
Eight hours to imagine my life,
Eight hours my machine the only one on
    loud as a bomb continually bursting.
No one knew I imagined myself all ages working there.
No one knew the instant I realized there were 24 presses
    and I was 24 years.
No one asked if I strolled the blackened corridors
    planting a kiss on the jaws of each monster.
No one guessed what the curled emptinesses without ends
    suspended from the ceiling on motionless conveyors
    in both directions to the vanishing point
        might hold for me,
Or the gondolas heaped with punched-out scrap,
Or words Chidiock Tychborn wrote
    the night before the chopping block
    recited by me to the giant metal darkness
        could he ever've imagined?
No one smelled what I smoked in the bathroom stall on my break.
No one saw me write Factories are our churches.
    We worship them more than forests.
    We worship them more than mountains.
    We'd rather drink from the tap than a stream.
    We'd rather open our refrigerator
        than a freshly killed deer.
No one saw me feeling my way back
    through the long dark pillared aisles
        of virgin cans with names we all know.
And when the foreman came by on his yellow scooter
    and from his lips I read LONG NIGHT
What could I do but smile
    for tears to dance round his corpse?

IX

Am I really from outerspace
Looking through super-x-ray telescope
Observing the life of one earthling
Wondering what it's like being him so much
    my thoughts are the same as his 24 years?

Or is it they captured me when my spaceship landed
        and doped me to forget the planet I'm from
        where I make a million bucks for this poem?
Amazing how they can program robots to imagine!
Making me think I'm alive! Making each memory seem real!
As if I was ever outside the factory even once since I was born!
As if there ever was a first day on the job so eager not to goof up!
Don't they think I can figure it out? Don't they think I know
        science can animate a cadaver? Don't they think I can think
            I've been made to think that I'm human?
Allowing me to flirt with this idea is the key,
        of course, to their control—
            so I can never be sure if they got me.
The sea? The Earth? The sky?
They've all been invented for my sake.
There's no History of Life, no Milky Way—
All there is is this factory stretching in every direction forever!
But it's not so bad—at least whatever computer card life
        they give you today really feels like it's happening,
            really feels like the one you've had all along.
And they even let you imagine they've invented some pill
        that'll make you feel while you factory
        that you're foresting or mountaining
            or tasting your first drink from a stream
Or the time and place and life of your choice—
Would you rather be Tyrannosaurus or Teratornis?
Would you rather be Neanderthal or Cro-Magnon?
How about Whitman? You haven't been him for a while.
Or Shakespeare? Remember how much fun it was
        the last time you wrote *Hamlet*?
Aren't you getting tired of discovering the Grand Canyon
        every day for the last two weeks?
Today why not discover fire
        or be Bruckner among the Sequoias?
Today why not yell "I quit!"
        simultaneously in every factory on Earth?
Or clap your hands and naked slaves appear
        and dance before your throne!
It's not so bad everyone's aware you're an experiment.
So what if the news runs a continual live broadcast
        of every second of your life?
Be grateful only the most carefully screened geniuses
        are selected to know you,
That everyone you speak to knows their lines in advance,
That even strangers must have degrees in automatonology,
And that right now the scientists are letting you think this.
They laugh. It's part of the hypothesis they're testing:

One of them bends to another and says—"Let's see
    what he says when I turn this knob."

O HUMAN CANNONBALLS OF EPIPHANY

Can cans ever be canned? Can the can-can ever be canned?
Can cantos of cannonfodder ever be canonized
    or the Canticle of Canticles of Cannabis
    never be cantabiled?
Can canasta in Canada canyons or going to the can
    never be cantata'd
    or can't it be canted
        because of cannibal cancer's uncanny candor
        making even cantaloupes cantankerous?
Hum-drum! Hum-drum! Hum-drum!
I should be paid for discovering America
    is committing suicide with factories!
I should be paid for wondering if I'm only a defect
    in the mass-production of zombies!
I should be paid for pondering if God packages universes
    the way I package lids!
I should be paid for combering if the sea ever gets tired
    of making the same sound!
I should be paid for writing *The Infinite Autobiography*
    of This Spot Through Eternity!
I should be paid to stand on this spot
    before America was discovered!
What do I win for singing—"No one can stand where I stand
    because my body is in the way"?
I should be paid to memorize the epic of every split-second!
I should be paid for hearing the chorus of fliptops
    popped all over the globe this instant!
I should be paid for turning fished-out cans upsidedown
    to count how many years falling leaves pour out!
How much do I get for watching the sunrise?
How much do I get for sleeping under the stars?
How much do I get for exploring the undiscovered
    oceans and continents
    and claiming them in Mescaline's name?
How much do these words want to work in my lines?
Is this poem worth more than a skyscraper?
This book worth more moolah than ever made?
I should be paid for listening to music
    better than virtuosos play!
I should be paid to play Kick the Can
    or tie cans to the newlydead's hearse!
I should be paid to fly a kite underground

careful not to snare it in the roots of trees!
What do I get for sisyphusing my face?
What do I get for glutting my sorrow
    on the wealth of the globéd peonies?
What do I get for knowing the hunting and gathering way of life
    represents 99% man's time on Earth?
Or for knowing the slaves who built the pyramids
    carved graffiti praising Pharaoh on the giant blocks of stone?
What do I get for knowing a billion dollar bills placed end to end
    would extend four times around the world
    and if you picked them up one per second
        it'd take 134 years?
I should be rich for knowing the answers
    to so many $64,000 Questions!
I should be rich for crying the Tarzan Cry
    that brings the skeletons of extinction to the rescue!

Before, I said—"There will always be room in my brain
    for the universe!"
Before, I said—"My soul will never be bludgeoned
    by the need to make money!"
Before, I said—"I will never cringe under the crack
    of the slavedriver's whip!"
Now my job is to murder the oceans!
Now my job is to poison the air!
Now my job is to chop down every tree!
I make food full of poison and say—"This is what you must buy!"
I'm in charge of torturing heretics
    and anyone who disagrees with the king!
I spend eight hours a day crucifying saviors!
I spend eight hours a day executing Lorcas!
I make slag heaps out of human souls!
I'm the first to go in the gas chamber after it's all over.
The corpses are piled on top of each other,
        the strongest on top, the weakest on bottom,
        all naked, many still twitching, still bleeding
            from noses and mouths,
        vomit, shit and piss befouling the agonied postures.
My job is to pull the gold teeth
    and shovel the bodies into the ovens.
Thanks to my work, Wolf Grizzly Eagle Whale
    and other deities in the pantheon of pantheism
        are no longer a threat to organized religion.
My job is to drop the Atomic Bomb on Hiroshima.
Twenty years later, asked would I do it again
    I say—"Yes."

O pay me for receiving the prophecies
     of the maggots of other worlds!
Pay me for the planets where before I was born
     I sang lullabies from my mother's vagina!
Let me be paid for bringing into Poetry
     penises and vaginas that will give us the visions
          we have wanted them to all along!
Let me be paid for rolling up my shirtsleeves and worshipping
     the ejaculations of joy!
O I should be paid to give blowjobs to boys,
     one hundred a day for the rest of my life!
And girls should be tickled pink for me to lick their clits
     till flying saucers come with frankincense and myrrh!
Eureka! I will make my fortune from plagiarizing death!
I will take the words from its mouth and it will not care!
I should be paid to say everyone's job is enlightenment!
I should be paid to run naked through the sprinkler
     the hottest day of summer!
I should be paid to lie in a canoe
     and drift over the lake all day!
What does it profit me to discover the pyramid
     of cans in the supermarket?
I demand to know how much sphincter gets
     staring brown daggers at its reflection!
How many smackers the tuckered-out eardrums?
How many frogskins the herculean heart
     and hardworking gonads?
Where are my royalties for discovering the telephone?
     And didn't I invent applause?
How many yachts and racehorses is that worth?
How many mansions? How many limousines
     for going over the Niagara of Last Words on a tightrope?
O pay me for saying if 75 feet represents the age of the Earth
     each step I take equals 100 million years!
O pay me for saying I could live the rest of my life
     on the money it costs to make one 500-pound bomb!
O pay me for saying every five days one million more humans
     on planet!
O pay me for discovering the origin of writing
     was to keep track of wealth and slaves!
O pay me for saying children who worked 12 hours a day
     were so tired they fell asleep with food in their mouths!
O pay me for showing adults in factories
     as tragic as child labor!
O pay me eight hours a day to do nothing
     but make bombscare phonecalls!

O pay me to say a poem is the best way
        to blow up a factory!
How many mediums of exchange do I get
        for getting higher than ever?
The cry of the eagle gives me a million!
The taste of wild berries gives me a million!
The smell of black locusts gives me a million!
The feeling swimming naked gives me a million!
I'm rich with all the visions opening cocoons afford!
A billionaire of reincarnations that can never be bankrupt!
O pay me to dress up as Santa
        and go down the Auschwitz chimneys!
O pay me for using so many exclamation points!
        Each worth more than a skyscraper!
O pay me for crushing a can in each fist!
Workaday! Workaday! Workaday!
Pilfer your livelong life away!
How can I think of quittin' when dis is moh fuhn
        dhan goin down da Big Muddy on a raf wif a runaway?

I guess I should tell you I'm really a zillionaire
        doing slave work just to see what it's like—
Or wait a minute, is it that I took some drug
        that makes me think I'm a zillionaire who took some drug
        to forget he's a zillionaire to see what doing slave
                work is like?

O pay me for knowing they let me say this.
For picturing how the control panel in robotfactory headquarters
        reacts,
How it flashes and the dials jump when I say
        the scientists are pleased with their creation.
One of them reads from the tickertape each word as I write it.
"Hey, listen to this," he smirks—
"I should be paid to say death restores us to soil
        no matter how unenlightened we are:
All melt in the mouth of the earth:
Each one is scrumptious to the critters
        to whom corpses taste good:
Each corpse a gift to the ground
        for roots to open into everything beyond them,
Opening slowly as the Colorado unwrapped the Grand Canyon
        till once more you're dreaming of gifts beneath the tree:
So don't bother complimenting death.
        Flattery will get you nowhere."
The scientists can't keep from clapping.
One of them bends to another and whispers—

"Remember when he raved about the laureate of blowjobs?"
"No, but is it true he said he got lost
        counting all the boyhoods he had?"

                            X

O thinking so much makes me weary.
Maybe I should pretend the masters
Nodding their heads in the invisible auditorium
        in which continual dialogues are held
        on the progress of my computerized soul
            are only a dream.
Maybe if I just stop thinking and look at the machines—
        the way the lids pour out like suicide battalions,
        the way I pretend to check for defects every so often,
        the way I shove enough in the bag like this,
        the way I stand the filled bag on end like this,
        the way I fold over the top and tape it like this,
        the way the rows of 'em rise on the skid like this—
MMMMMM, that's better, now I'm myself again—
All I have to do is stand here
        and package factories as they come from the press—
Factories that make cans.
Factories that make the machines that make cans.
Factories that make the machines that make the machines
        that make cans.
Factories that make factories.
Factories that make factories that make factories
        that make everything that goes into cans.
Factories that make can openers.
Factories that make electric can openers.
Factories that make candy and canoes.
Factories that make candles and candelabras
        and incandescent lightbulbs.
Factories that make cuckoo-clock canaries.
Industries of canned laughter, canned applause,
        canned music.
Telephone factories, television factories,
        radio, stereo, tape recorder factories,
        refrigerator, stove and toilet factories.
Telescope factories, microscope factories,
        film, camera, movie screen factories,
        jukebox, roulette wheel and slot machine factories.
Industries of nuts! Industries of bolts!
Industries of bulldozers, roadgraders, steamshovels,
        cement mixers, steamrollers, jackhammers,

pile drivers and wrecking cranes!
Every building and street in every dot on the map
        and all the highways between them
        constructed from products of multitudinous factories!
Factories of cars and toy cars,
        trucks and toy trucks, trains and toy trains,
        planes and toy planes, ships and toy ships,
        spaceships and toy spaceships!
Factories of money and factories of play money!
Factories of all that money can buy!
Mass production of pricetags!
Assembly lines of cash registers!
Application and paycheck form factories!
Lunchbucket and thermosbottle factories!
Earplug and timeclock and alarmclock factories!
        and self-winding watches given factoryhands at retirement
        made in what factories!
Factories of lady's ware, men's ware, children's ware, baby's ware,
        silverware, copperware, tinware, glassware,
        stoneware, woodenware, earthenware, plasticware,
        furniture, souvenirs, knickknacks, novelties,
        gizmos, geegaws, glockenspiels and greeting cards!
Ambulances, police cars, and buses from factories!
Fire engines, fire escapes, and matches from factories!
Sirens, foghorns, steamwhistles, rockguitars, grandpianos,
        every instrument in the orchestra including the baton
        and the concert hall all hatched from myriad factories!
O every record I love I know where you come from!
O cookiecutters! birdhouses! buddhastatues and plastic vomit!
        I know where you come from!
                O awls, axes, adzes, augers,
                barrels, bearings, bellows, brads,
                crowbars, corkscrews, crucibles, calipers,
                dumbbells, dollies, dibbles, drills,
                exhausts, excelsior, forceps, faucets,
                gauges, gouges, gaskets, goggles,
                hammers, hammocks, hangers, hoists,
                irons, icepicks, jewels, jacks,
                keels, kilns, levels, ladles, lathes,
                mops, muzzles, mattresses, microphones,
                nails, neon, napalm, ouija boards,
                pistons, pitchforks, pliers, puncheons,
                quivers, quoits, ratchets, rounces,
                radar, roachclips, scales, scalpels,
                snorkels, stencils, shovels, shoetrees,
                squeegees, tweezers, trophies, trocars,
                tampons, trampolines, uniforms, umbrellas,

vises, valves, wormgears, wrenches,
wigs, wire, yardsticks, zippers—
I know where you come from!
And I know where the machines that make you come from!
And all the letters for alphabet soup!
Breweries, canneries, tanneries, creameries,
(Name me something not come from Factory)
Brassworks, gasworks, refineries, binderies,
Plants that make barberpoles, barberchairs,
dentistchairs, electric chairs,
electric knives, electric fans,
electric shavers, electric blenders,
electric blankets, electric fireplaces,
electric toothbrushes, electric eyes!
Everything in the Sears Roebuck Catalogue
is not from the legendary herds of buffalo!
Typewriter sweatshops! Motorcycle sweatshops!
Revolving door sweatshops! Intercom sweatshops!
Mass production of straitjackets!
Mass production of bombs!
Vast spectrum of death machines of land, sea and sky!
More bullets than people who ever lived!
More bayonets than books ever written!
Better machines for killing invented so fast
they're obsolete before used!
So much an hour mass production of crosses and flags!
Purple-heart gristmills! Basket-case gristmills!
Industries of homicidal deceit:
glamorizing cigarets no different than Nazis
telling Jews gas chambers are shower rooms!
Millions of new cradles and coffins each year!
Corpses rolling down the conveyor belt of the funeral factory!
Slaughterhouse factories and all the tools of the slaughterhouse:
cleavers, bludgeons, meat-hooks, sticklers!
Fish, mammal, bird factories! Fruit, vegetable, grain factories!
Every bite processed in factories!
Strip me naked, abandon me in deepest woods in Canada—
my body still from Factory!
My flesh flesh of what factories raised from birth
and murdered for my mouth!
Supermarket Factories! University Factories!
Hospital Factories! Prison Factories!
Death Factories!
Stop! Don't you think I get the point?
All the floors of the department store
and the elevator girl telling me
the goods on each as the doors open?

Is it necessary to list
        every machine necessary to extract raw materials
        and every machine necessary to transport them
        and every machine necessary to transform them
                into iron, steel, aluminum,
        and everything made from iron, steel, aluminum,
        and every machine necessary to make it?
What do I get for unveiling the machinery that makes
        footballs, baseballs, basketballs, tennisballs,
        bowlingballs, billiardballs, pingpongballs, snowmobiles,
        boxinggloves, golfclubs, sailboats, surfboards,
        scubagear, bathtubs, and easychairs?
Must we see the slaves behind every device of recreation and leisure?
Must we see the slaves behind every laborsaving device?
(Do you think it's trite to call them slaves?
Are you only a company man for Literature
        slaving on the disassembly line of criticism?
Are you only a cog in the Poetry Factory?
How many poems by Zinjanthropus
        appear in your Immortal Anthology?)
Wheelbarrow factories! Kitchen sink capitalisms!
Staplegun generalissimos! Toothpick presidents!
Paperclip czars! Linoleum pharaohs!
Punchpress emperors! Pushbutton potentates!
Monopoly millionaires! Deodorant billionaires!
Electricity trillionaires! Computer quadrillionaires!
Quintillionaires of wood! Sextillionaires of rock!
Septillionaires of plastic! Octillionaires of oil!
Nonillionaires of flesh! Decillionaires of Oblivion!
        The exact number of pennies ever made!
        The exact number of papercups ever made!
        The exact number of number two pencils ever made!
More rope! More tape! More pipe! More fence!
More wallets! More purses! More needles! More thread!
More envelopes! More stamps! More brushes! More paint!
More boxes! More bottles! More screws! More screwdrivers!
More washingmachines! More airconditioners! More vacuum cleaners!
        More flashlight batteries!
Dynamos stretching to the horizon and still not enough!
More generators! More blastfurnaces! More concrete! More antennae!
Capitalisms of thumbtacks and thumbscrews!
Stockholders in tongue-depressors and rectal thermometers!
Manufacturers of lawnmowers, snowblowers, toenail clippers
        and machetes!
World's largest producers of arrows, slingshots, fishhooks,
        riflesights, decoys, traps, and raccoon death-cry calls!
Peddlers of pills and more pills and pill containers

and prescription forms!
Industries for the Blind! Industries for the Retarded!
Where artificial flavor and color are made!
Where artificial flowers and grass are made!
Where artificial eyes and arms and legs are made!
    and wherever they make boobytraps!
    and wherever they make tiddlywinks!
    and wherever they make doors and doorknobs
        and doorbells and hinges and locks and keys!
Corporations of bulletproof vests and silencers!
Corporations of blowtorches, rivetguns and girders!
(And where do dildoes and bathyspheres fit in?)
Every breath more parkingmeters and bankvaults
    and armored trucks and turnstiles
    and wedding rings and vagina dolls
    and rubbers and rubberbands
    and rubber rafts and lifepreservers
    and thingamabobs and thingamadoodles
    and gargle and garbage trucks
        and garbage cans
        and sprinkling cans
        and aerosol cans
        and "Eat" signs
        and "Stop" signs
        and "No Trespassing" signs
    and switchboards and turbines
    and conveyor belts of conveyor belts!
And the world's largest producers of machineguns and chainsaws!
And 20,000 a day extermination factory of Auschwitz!
And one billion gallons of gasoline burned in California each month!
And 38 cigarets inhaled every day in New York City
    just by breathing the air!
And even you, backpacks, compasses, and maps of the wild?
    must you be from factories?
Et tu mountain climbing gear?
And even icecream and kaleidoscopes
    and bubblewands and balloons
        and swingsets and teetertotters
        and yoyos and marbles
        and frisbees and skateboards
        and pinwheels and merrygorounds
        and beanies with propellers
        and the hall of mirrors?
Must we see the slaves behind every toy of our childhood?
Must we see the gypped lives behind the pantheon of laughs?
    O souls flophoused by factories!
    O geniuses imbeciled by factories!

O enlightenment shoplifted by factories!
Copying machine factories! Calculating machine factories!
Vending machine factories! Change machine factories!
Humans spending their lives making lipstick or eyeshadow!
Humans spending their lives making crystal balls or fortune cookies!
Humans spending their lives making calendars or blindman canes!
Working your way up to foreman in the insecticide factory!
Working your way up to employment manager in the squirtgun factory!
Working your way up to the top in the pay toilet factory!
    40 years making piggybanks!
    480 months making burglar alarms or handcuffs!
    2000 weeks making wind chimes, wind machines
        or wind-up toys!
    10,400 days of your life
        making stopwatches or metronomes!
    83,200 hours of your life
        making miniature replicas of Rodin's Thinker!
    4,992,000 minutes of your life
        gluing the hemispheres of globes together!
    299,952,000 seconds of your life
        cranking out the links of chains!

XI

What have I forgotten?
How many more should I name?
Is there no end to this list?
Factories that make newspapers every day
    and all the job openings in the want ads?
Factories that make yellow pages and all the factories
    in the yellow pages of every city on Earth?
More factories than words in this poem!
More than all the odes in praise of marijuana or blowjobs
    ever written!
More than all the miles I'll ever backpack or canoe
    pristine primordial lake-forest-peak wilderness!
Even if I toured every factory there is
    and each tour lasted only a minute,
        it would take centuries!
No second of my life in which slaves are not slaving!

Don't tell me it's trite to say they are slaves!
Don't tell me it's banal to say every second counts!
Don't tell me I use too many exclamation points!
(Can there ever be too many exclamation points!)
Don't tell me it's boring to see all the ways

humans make human sacrifice of their lives!
Don't tell me how leaves are factories!
   or of the factories of my bones and balls!
I have milked by hand! I know the milking machine joke!
I know I smell with an olfactory system!
I know mitochondria are the powerhouses of cells!
I don't need to be reminded honey is the busywork of bees!
I don't need to be told the Sun is the Factory of Light!

Death from the cornucopia of Factories!
Death from the stupor, stupor, stupor of the daily grind!
Massacre of land, sea and sky by stupendous machines!
Mutilation of souls beyond recognition!
Factories that have actually made enough bombs
   to blow up the Earth any second!
Factories of the death-cry of America and Mankind
   and every Livingkind on my planet!
Factories whose noise numbs the ear to Poetry!
Factories whose God is not Love unless Love is Money!
Factories that make millions of books that say—
   "Without factories we couldn't live.
Behind everything we need to survive is a machine.
Without factories you wouldn't be reading these words."
I draw lines from all the things I own
   to the factories that made them
   and from each factory to the homes of its slaves.
How long will it take me to work my whole life
   on each of the jobs in every factory on Earth?
Ah, epics could be written in each of them.
How would this all be different
   if I'd worked where they make
      kites or fireworks,
      teaballs or plumbbobs,
      mannikins or sledgehammers,
      tuning forks or cattleprods,
      flamethrowers or shoppingcarts,
      wheelchairs or hearingaids,
      paper or fountain pens,
      pacifiers or puppets,
      or poured sand into hourglasses
      passing by on conveyor belt?

Maybe I won't be able to write unless I work in a factory!
Even if I get rich I'll have to buy a machine
   for the turret of my castle
      so I can go there and scribble
      to its ravenous roar:

Except to make money,
We are no longer responsible for our survival.
We don't have to hunt or kill our own food.
We don't have to build our own houses or tools,
        know how to make fire without matches,
                make our own clothes or canoes,
                be our own heroes, doctors, priests,
        and teach our children how to smell the weather.
Once there were no cities or farms.
Once there were no factories or slaves.
Once everything ever made in factories did not exist.
Is there no way to cut the umbilicus to factories?
No way to be born into a world not made in factories?
No way to unpledge this hopeless allegiance
        to suicide by factories?
Not one stream left where the water flows free
        of human junk from source to mouth?
No breath left to breathe anywhere
        untainted by exhaust pipes and smokestacks?
Is it too late to ask—"What good is it if we're immortal
        when we're bored with eternity even before we die?"
Is it time to begin to dream of the sphere in space
        where America exists before it was discovered?
What was I born for? What was I born for?
        Is this a Factory I see before me?

XII

Perhaps you've already stopped reading this poem,
Perhaps you want to get paid for reading this far.
Don't think I haven't caught you turning the pages
        to see how much longer it is to the end.
Don't think I haven't caught you
        looking at the clock.
How long does it take to write *I am growing old*?
What right do 24 years have to speak of age?

This poem does not want to die,
        but it is very tired now.
It has so many little children in it
        that want to go home,
That want to be told a story
        they can fall asleep halfway through—

Once, that day before the night I worked alone,
        past "No Trespassing" signs and barbed wire,

Smoking the last words of centuries
    amid birch, oak, shagbark and grosbeak song,
Exhaling into faces of trilliums and mosquitos,
    wanting everything to be high,
In a small clearing I did what I always wanted to do—
    stripped naked and shat—
My head and arms rising to the sun
    so that when they could reach no further
I felt what my body would never be again touch me for the last time,
    smelling in the 93 million mile rays my remains,
        my source,
And savoring the mystic perfume in that stench
(Perfume that can be called nothing but mystic)
And grabbing myself as if my hand were God
I pulled my life from my testicles up and out
    the shaft of my blazing erection—
        splendid arcs of semen
        glittering through the air—
Saying to my turds—"Be my past, be my boyish boyhoods
    small shap't and firmly carv'd, finely laid and sleek,"
And to my semen—"Be my future, my future opening mouth
    between legs spread with naked joy
        in the wavering leaf-shade
    where Indian Pipes and Moccasin Flowers
        are still fringed with dew."
An hour later Factory surrounded me.
A week later pilgrimage found no trace of my conversion.

XIII

What more can I say?
The day came as I knew it would,
The day that waited for me all along
    just as much as the machines waited,
Just as much as the day I was conceived
And all the days before I had to become a slave,
    before I was taught to spell money,
Before I understood my corpse
    and everything beyond the disappearance of my corpse
        waits for me,
And just as much as the end of this poem
Waited for me before the beginning of time
    and for whoever reads it
        after the extinction of clocks,
The day I would quit waited for me,
Waited for me to apply and be hired,

For the routines of slavery to be learned
    and the slow countdown of days
        to be endured,
For me, it waited, patiently, that day,
Waited for me to pick up my paycheck so many times,
To stare at the clock as I worked dreaming of quitting
    so many times,
To think of all the things as a man I did not want to be,
And for freedom to long for me patient as worms
    all the days before they are human again,
While the odyssey of eternity on this one spot in the universe
    contemplated itself—
While the infinite epic of each second in infinity
    touched me—
From the birth of the sun,
From the birth of the Earth,
From the birth of all life
    to the earliest men,
From the discovery of fire,
From the invention of tools,
From when each word was once a poem
    and what it was like to live at that time
        when all men hunted and killed their own food
    and carved the mammoth from the mammoth's tusk,
From the invention of farming and herding 10,000 years ago,
From the invention of writing 5000 years ago
    and printing 500 years ago,
From the first cities, from the first factories,
From the first swirl of the whirlpool
    whose vortex we spin in so fast
        no one knows anymore what will happen,
From having to stop writing these words every ten seconds
    to tube or bag the lids of cans
And how this incantation rose and still rises
    and will never stop rising
        from the catacombs of incomprehensible zombies!
And so, as I knew it would, the day came
When waiting in line to punch out it was for the last time,
When for the last time I would see the slaves
    race past me trying to be first
        from carlot to freeway to bar
    to drink till they dreamed they were free,
When for the last time I would follow the way home
    past all the factories that lay between
        giant in the aura of their power at midnight
    through the empty streets in the rain.

How could I have known months after I quit
        as I lay waiting for sleep
                my ears would still echo that roar,
        the din of presses and minsters?
How could I have known I'd bolt from bed at all hours
        gasping—"I'm late!"
                only to realize I quit long ago
        the din of presses and minsters?
How could I have known years later driving past Factory
        the most seductive night of summer,
                seeing all the lights on, the smokestacks billowing,
        I would say—"Just think, people are working right now"
                and let the best grass I ever smoked
        remember me there
                in the din of presses and minsters?

How can you kill yourself if you're already dead?
How can you kill yourself with something made in a factory?
How can you kill yourself before embracing the invisible tree
        above every stump?
How can you kill yourself before the arena
        packed with your future lives
        cheers you on?
Before, I said—"If you've already stopped reading this
        you'll never know how it ends!"
Before, I said—"As long as there are slaves
        this poem will never end!
        As long as there are factories
        my metamorphosed remains
        will continue to ponder
        the wasted lives!"
Before, I said—"Poets should be paid to skydive naked
        to all the doors where slaves go in,
                proclaiming from the robes of their chutes
        how the corpse waits in the man
        the man waits in the boy
        the boy waits in the child
        the child waits in the baby
                waiting all the orgasms of ancestors
                to be fucked into being
        patient as maggots are patient
        all the days they must wait
                before they become human again,
        before they elegize again the wasted lives,
        before they can proclaim once more
                the immortality of death!"

What am I waiting for? I am free to go.
The next shift has begun. Why am I standing here
    watching them work?
There's nothing I can say they will hear.
There's nothing more to be seen.
I have shown the gouged-out souls.
I have shown the castrated souls.
I have shown the souls torn limb from limb.
I have shown the disemboweled souls.
Now you know the difference between hunting for money
    and hunting the woolly rhinoceros.
I have performed the adagio of the opening cocoon.
Because of me Poetry knows my childhood
    stacked coins into dank castles of smell.
Because of me Poetry knows it took 500 million man-hours
    to build the highest building in the world.
Because of me from now on every factory-made object
    unceasingly mantras—"I was made by a slave!"
I have not made my fortune in gravedigging machines
    or garbage disposals.
I'm no plutonium tycoon or entrepreneur of nerve gas.
I'll never spend my life creating ways to make poison taste better
    and sell more.
From mountaintops I have gazed
    more than the money of all time.
From the start the rainbow has arched to my palate
    the promise of these words.
I have inherited the earth.
I have inherited the sky.
I have tinkered this handmade craftsmanship
    in my own little shop.
The Epic of Zombies has come from my hand.
The Spectacle of Millions Slowly Tortured to Death Their Whole Lives
    has come from my hand.
There aren't enough libraries for the screams.
There aren't enough banks for the tears.
Can't you smell the putrescent lives?
The wasted lives, can't you smell them?
I've escaped unburied from the untold miles of genocide tickertape
    gibbered from the monoliths of greed.
I've escaped from the slaughterhouse of souls.
I've closed my eyes by the machines
    and imagined I stood in the thunder and spray
        of the unknown falls
Crying—"Every city that exists will disappear!
    Every nation that exists will disappear!"
Don't ask me how. Don't ask me why.

All I know is numberless planets
        have realized Utopia.
All I know is there will be no ghost dance
        for the nuclear bomb.
All I know is no one will timemachine to our time
        to work in a tollway tollbooth
                giving correct change their whole life
        to car after car.

O millions of sanddollars be left by the tide!
O children radiant with soot emerge from the mines at last!
O inside the pyramid stand on the spot where you look up
        and see through to the stars!
Freedom! Liberty! Deliverance!
(Am I the primitive man who invented those words?)
I proclaim the resurrection of everyone who is dead
        that is still alive!
No one will have giant keys in their backs any longer!
No one will cut themselves and find clockwork inside any longer!
From now on no one will die discovering they had not lived!
        No more strangleholds! No more strangleholds!
Ungag our souls!! Unstrangle our souls!! Unsmother our souls!!
        I PROCLAIM THE EXTINCTION OF FACTORIES!!!
Already they are gone. Not a trace remains.
        I can hardly believe I am so powerful.
There are no more slaves! No one knows anymore what money is!
The utmost passion of eternity feels itself in every human being!
        Everything ever made in factories has disappeared.
Once more a squirrel can travel from the Atlantic to the Mississippi
        from tree to tree without touching the ground.
Once more the buffalo and passenger pigeon.
Once more wilderness Earth that is heaven.
Once more wilderness men that are gods.
I gaze down on the untouched continent.
How many centuries have fallen away?
        Is this America?
                What should I call it?
Am I the first man
        to set foot
                on this land?

Here is the door.
I'll open it now.
All I have to do
        is open it
        and leave.
For all I know
        the city will no longer be there

52

and I'll walk into the absolute forest—
Machines are not trees, machines are not clouds,
Lids advancing forever are neither streams nor lapping shores,
Clocks are not moons, moons are not coins,
Coins are not the view from the mountaintop,
      jobs are not sunrise,
      work is not dawn:
The Miracle of Factory passes from my life!
"Working at Continental Can Co." R!I!P!

Like a kite played higher and higher
Pulls more gently as it gets smaller and smaller
     until it's hardly there, only a dot,
        and tugs like the memory
    of some unrequited caress,
So the years have come between me and that time,
     those factorydays of my past,
        those futile days of my life,
But not until all factories are turned into playgrounds in moonlight,
Not until all applicants for factories must memorize this poem
    to be hired,
Not until I'm hired to dress like a grasshopper and fiddle
     "O the world owes me a livin'"
        to the nation of ants
Will I let go of the string.

And when the time comes to let go
Let the last thing I remember be
    the night when the power failed,
When the monsters that even now
     are preaching the same circular words
        that will outlive us all failed,
When everything stopped and went dark,
How in the sudden vast silence of factory
    I heard my own voice for the first time,
And crouching at the feet of the machines
In that dark broken only by exit lights
    how I closed my eyes
Wondering if when I opened them
    I would be 15,000 years ago
Beginning in the flickering of my torch
    to paint the antler'd dancer
        on the vault of my cave.

The Puberty of Smell

If the second before pulling the trigger you remember me,
            remember me smelling lilacs,
How every time smelling lilacs I remember
The time my mescalined olfactory system
            caught on the early morning breeze
            the full-blossomed and blossoming lilacs
                    at Big Smoky Falls,
How my nose approached like a boy
            discovering his cock feels so good
            he can't help crying out,
How circling the tree at nose level
            caressing with my nose
            those purple clouds of fragrance
I experienced where I smell inside my skull
            above my mouth and under my eyes
                    in the very center
            my nose's first orgasm,
Not caring if anyone saw my abandon—
Though no one was there, no one but birds
            and songs the sun rises in them
                    and the falls and the song of the falls
            and the song of mosquitos
                    I gave my blood to with joy—
And even if I didn't think then
            of the scent between pubescent legs,
Or remember my boyhood cock no longer exists
            to caress breasts of early morning dreams,
I saw them opening,
            all opening and opening themselves
And glowing in the sun's first rays,
            lifting themselves to the sun
            in the just-felt breeze
As if they'd waited,
As if everything in the Universe had waited
Till I came, till I could smell them opening,
            my nose caressed by those blossoms, those lilacs,
            those clusters of fragrance and the living color
                    called purple,
As I opened and closed my eyes with my breathing,
Every so often remembering where I was,
Remembering I had a face and that face had a nose—
            for didn't it seem to me then
            all I was was that smell?

Jim—
Even if you've already killed yourself,
When the time comes you have my name and I have yours,
        write this for me,
Or when next you're about to pull the trigger,
Remember in that second before you discover
        if you can hear the shot
That for a few grains of the hourglass
        this was me—
That I too had no choice,
        drawn by the smell irresistible,
My nose approaching like the lover
        who believes no one on earth can love
            more passionately—
Remember me then smelling so hard
As if I were the first to aroma
        this peculiar translation of corpses,
As if I were the first to make love to lilacs,
As if I were entering strange houses of early morning
        drawn toward sleeping boys to hold lilac sprigs
        to nostrils of their dreams,
As if I'd discovered the answer
        to all the questions the Universe inside my skull
        could ask.
And so, in the second before you blow out your brain,
        when you look into the gun and feel
            where the hole in your head will be,
Remember you were immortal before you were born,
        that even before this poem
            your suicide must be fragrant as lilacs,
And always remember in that morning the color of lilacs
How I smelled them till I could smell them no more,
        withdrawing, fulfilled and wondering
If you went to those lilacs at Big Smoky Falls
        you'd be surprised they had no smell
        because I must've inhaled it all,
Wondering if I'd smelled those purple clouds so well
        if you inhaled from my nose
        you could smell them now.

The Dark Inside a Life

To learn how to die cut down a tree,
Watch how so many years fall.
You don't need to have planted it for it to be your life.

You know countless trees have grown
        and will grow where this tree falls.
Everyone alive now will be underground
        and will have gone from roots, branches and leaves
        to roots, branches and leaves many times.
You've seen how the seed of a tree
        can rise from the pit of a stump.
Wherever your feet touch earth
        you know you are touching
        where something has died or been born.

Count the rings and stand on the stump and stretch your arms
        to the sky.
Think only because it was cut down could you do this.
You are standing where no one has stood
        but the dark inside a life
        that many years.

View from Imp Lake Lookout

Before taking Mescaline at Imp Lake
I drove up the dirt road to the lookout the map told me was there
To find only the platform where it stood remained,
And standing where the tower once stood,
      looking up being my view,
It seemed the lifetime of the tower and the tower's view
        and all the feet that ever climbed the winding stairs to the top
        imagined me then:
The ranger deciding here was the spot for the tower,
The tower in the architect's brain, the factory fashioning its parts,
The shipment of parts, the making of the forest road
      and the Tower signpost and parkinglot
      and path from parkinglot to the tower's base,
And the tower's construction, the unfolding blueprint,
      trees falling, girders rising, putting in the steps,
      securing the viewing platform, the foreman's final OK,
      machinery and workers driving away, the money it cost
      changing hands, the silence returning once more,
And all the feet that climbed the lifespan of the tower—
      how many years how many footsteps echoing upward
      toward the vista expanding in every direction
      each footstep up the number of steps upward
      50, 100, 150, 200 feet high,
Dawn, noon, dusk, night, spring, summer, fall, winter,
      the continual autobiography of the sky—
Babies carried up in their mothers' arms,
Children who can climb only one step at a time,
Girls two steps at a time racing friends to the top
      nonstop giggling out-of-breath,
Boys on top holding the gobbing contest or the pissing contest
      or balancing on guard rails on a dare,
Fathers yelling at kids to be careful,
Those afraid to go all the way up,
Those too old reading "Climb at your own risk"
      who climb up anyway,
Those gone to the top for blowjob in moonlight,
      or fucking in sunrise,
Those curious what makes pretending to throw each other off
      so much fun,
Epileptics, amputees, morons, deformed persons, those who are blind,
      and fetuses umbilicusing the view from their mothers' eyes,
Those blindfolded by friends, not told where they're going,
      led to the top and the blindfold unpinned,
And those who looked from the top but never really saw the view,

All walks of life walking upward, all different outlooks looking out,
All the occupations in the yellow pages rising above the trees
        and the dream of the job that's living on a tower
        and looking for fires rising with them,
And those lamenting the extinction of crow's-nests, lighthouses
        and lookout towers,
And the one wondering if someday the tower will stand
        surrounded by rushhour megapolis
        (quaint reminder of Upper Michigan wilds
        extant in the shadow of highrise apartments),
And the one wondering how long to stay on top
        because friends are restless and want to move on,
And the one who believes himself unworthy to go up
        till all the woods seen from the view have walked through him,
And don't forget the one who goes up to see what the forest
        that'll take Mescaline in him looks like to a hovering bird,
And don't forget Mescaline climbing the tower
        in the shape of a human being,
And don't forget Mescaline climbing steps of epiphany
        in the human brain,
And connoisseurs of wilderness towers
        who pilgrimage from towertop to towertop,
Those who like being noisy on top,
Those to whom even a whisper is sacrilege,
And all who returned again and again,
Who climbed these winding stairs each year of their life,
Who became friends with the view
        and gloried in the possibilities of Tower—
Sunrise on top, Sunset on top,
        star study, cloud study, bird study on top,
Thanksgiving on top, kite flying on top,
        milkweedpods, waterballoons, soapbubbles on top,
        snowmen on top, trampoline on top, tai chi or yoga
        or Auschwitz photos on top, flute or harp
        or helicoptered piano on top, photography on top,
        topography on top, Mescaline on top,
        soliloquy on top, suicide on top,
        jacking off on top in berserk thunderstorm,
Shouting your name loud as you can from cupped hands
        and cupping your ears for an echo,
Learning the view by heart,
Dancing the view turning in circles fast as you can,
Scribbling "inexhaustible view" in your notebook
        or "the vista that invites the eye into its distance"
        or "the panorama expanding before me further than I can see,"
Dropping a boulder from on top close as possible
        to your friend's head as he lies on the ground watching it fall

to savor the shock of his body hitting the ground if he jumped,
Smearing the steps with honey and dressing in clothes made of bacon
        crouched on top for the dream-bear,
Or wearing costumes of other times and lands as you climb,
        or smoking a joint each step of the way,
Or digging secret passageway from the tower's base to your basement,
Or performing the ceremony of climbing in fog
        when from the base the top of the tower is lost
        and when from the top not even the tops of trees can be seen,
And all those wilderness tourists who considered the tower their throne,
        anyone else there a trespasser on their solitude kingdom,
And how many times hoping to find no one there,
        on reaching the last breathless step
        someone's already conducting the view from the podium,
And finally, the poet who imagined me writing this poem,
        who looked down where I stand now looking up...
And so, looking up at the towerless sky,
        I wondered,
Is this all that's left of the view?

(If there is an audience and I'm reading this
        it should be from a tower.
In a room if this poem succeeds,
        walls become lakes, chairs become trees,
                200 feet of tower rise me above them,
        ceiling becomes sky and I'm alone once more
And each of you is alone on some wilderness dream-risen tower.)

But the map still shows the tower is there
And I keep seeing the others who will drive up the dirt road
Only to look up from the base the tower was secured to and rested on
Wishing for the view the top commanded
        to command them
From days no one was there and the view could enjoy being alone,
Days of continuous wind sung through the winding stairs
        when no one rose but the snow,
        when no one looked down but the hawk
        on the wind-tossed waves of pine,
To the weekend stampede, every step with a foot on it
        like the line before a casket
        waiting to take a last look—
And every photo taken on top looks at us,
And graffiti carved everywhere hands could reach considers us,
And the recording never made of all the words spoken on top
        listens to us,
And the movie never made of dismantling the tower dismantles us,
And the lifetime of the ever-changing shadows of the tower

overshadows us all.

I think I'll climb into the sky
      and look from the lookout awhile.
My feet should be able to find where each step was
      and just where to turn to go up the next flight.
My eyes should be ready by now
      to see what the view has to show.
I want to watch a few centuries go by,
      houses growing closer one by one,
Each in its turn replaced by buildings
      replaced in their turn by skyscrapers,
And the view from the skyscraper risen from this spot,
      and the proud who scorn elevator
      for stairs,
And the crowds no less mysterious
      yet no less terrifying
      than those in the city I always return to
      wondering if I will always return.
And not till the poet stands where the skyscraper stood
And looking up points out the view
Will I be ready to climb down the invisible stairs of the air
      to be put in his mouth and swallowed
      and called with a whisper—
      Mescaline.

Staff

I have worn smooth with the grip of my hand
        branches found by the trail,
Caught by my eye and lifted,
Thrown in the air and caught by my hand and tested—
        if it's not too long,
        if it's not too short,
        if it feels just right,
I say to myself— "This is my staff!"
        and thump the ground with its end.

Carry me far! Take me where I must go!
Miles away from miles away from every road,
        every house, every human voice
        or voice of machine,
Through woods I love,
Past lakes where no one is,
Beyond where the footpath ends,
        up where the mountains glow
        and the sky has never been breathed!

And should I again among crutches and canes
        umbrellas and books under arms
Walk in the skyscraper's shadow,
It will be with my staff,
It will be in clothes smelling of campfires
        and moss,
And if myriad strangers stare
        curious, suspicious, indignant,
I'll grip my staff tight as I pass
        and let wilderness speak through my mouth
How the feel of this staff
        puts me in touch with the Gods,
Transports me back through the eras,
To the epochs of staff-bearing men,
To the heritage of this wand
        of power and prophecy.

Isn't the only way to write
        with a pencil this size?
For words to be so large
        you must get out your compass,
And the only way to write mountain
        is to climb to the top?

Numberless possible staffs
	wait on the forest floor,
Or fallen from high trees
	caught in their lower branches,
Or resting against a stump
	as if someone left them there.

My walking stick urges me on,
	takes my hand like a friend,
Comforts me, steadies me
	over rough terrain,
Beyond where it's ever been mapped,
Where no human ever set foot,
Following the voice of the stream
	up where the mountains glow
	and the sky has never been breathed!

Enskyment

Imagine being buried in air,
       in the light blue earth of the sky,
Slowly lowered into thin atmospheres
       on pulleys of evaporation
While shovels of clouds shovel clouds over you
       and you hear far away
The last spadefuls of steeples and fireworks
       and clapping and laughter
And birdsong and forests and mountains
       all scooped on your immense grave of sky!

Imagine those heavenly maggots:
       lost kites, lost balloons,
Seeds we make wishes on,
       butterflies, fireflies,
Wingspreads of vultures,
       and all the nibbling stars.
And branches of trees really roots and roothairs?
       And rainbows really the tunnels of moles?
And earthworms peeping from their holes
       really birdbeaks probing the earth?

What exquisite decay!
All the warmth the sun gives as it melts you!
All those tons of cirrus, stratus, cumulonimbus!
       Skyquakes of lightning!
Your flesh unpetalling in downpours!
Your body become all sunset and ozone,
       delicate rumbles of vanishing thunder!
Till the aroma of sky after rain
       and earth after rain
Is all that's left of your corpse!

First Drink from a Stream

Into the map feet-first floating downward
I descend toward the first stream I shall drink from
To stand one foot on each bank
With water rushing beneath me.

Before dipping hands brought together
I would whet my thirst with knowing
How many lips searching for lips
Had to come this far for a kiss.

And purer than water is pure,
And cooler than water is cool,
Is the flow of this liquid imagining
Down my esophagus.

Beyond the postures of all the ages
Of animals bending to sip, I kneel,
Lifting in cupped hands
What began and will always begin
From clouds down mountains
Rushing before me and after me
Equal infinities, the living song
Old as water is old
And older than the first boy
Who could suck his own cock
And cupping balls drink from himself
The freshness.

And swallowing I would be quenched
Knowing how little of all the water
That ever feels its way
Through the bed of this stream
Is needed to slake my thirst.
And knowing no name for this stream
I will call it after myself,
As sometimes in my quietest time
I whisper my name to myself
Looking up where I came from
Curious what cupped hands dip from the sky
For one handful of my voice.

from **REWORKING WORK**

Written After Learning Slaves in Ancient Greece and Rome Had 115 Holidays a Year

Instead of creating better murder weapons
    to "protect" ourselves,
Better create loving boys and girls
    who become loving women and men.
Instead of a higher standard of living
    why not a higher standard of loving?
Why not a higher standard
    of getting high?
No more brainwashed robotzombies!
No more socialization lobotomies!

Thoreau could live a whole year
    on money from working 6 weeks.
We canned ourselves in concentration camps
    called cities
And in buildings and room where we work.
We have become hermetically sealed containers.
The can of today is the wilderness that was.
The can-to-be is the wilderness that is.

As Oscar Wilde said: "Work is the curse
    of the drinking man."
As Stan Jones said: "It's not what the machine makes,
    but what the machine makes you."
As Virgil said: *Deus nobis haec otia facet:*
    "A god has granted us this idleness."
As Lessing said: "Let us be lazy in everything
    except in loving and drinking,
    except in being lazy."

Should cans stop being made?
Should all factories immediatly close down?
What solution do you provide? If everyone's a poet
    and no one works, how do we survive?
The way St. Theresa survived on Light?
Love becomes a full-time job?
But where do we get the money
    to pay people not to work?

Slaves in ancient Greece and Rome
       had 115 holidays a year!
Hey, wait a minute, that makes us
       more slaves than them!

The Way I Figure It

The way I figure it
No one should be a slave.
Everyone should be free.
When I think of my own life
       I think Wow,
Already I've worked over five years
       in factories!
For working that long I deserve
       the rest of my life
       to be a paid vacation.
Then I start thinking of my mother
       and brother and sister
       and friends
Chained to jobs they have to put up with,
Yet my father being dead is free from all that,
But when I think how he only got
       a three week vacation every year,
Or how the 12-hour day 6-day workweek for pittance
       was once taken for granted,
And even now people get a one-week vacation
       in their 20s or 30s
Or a two-week vacation
       in their 40s or 50s...
I've got to make up for them by golly!
Why, every day a person works in a factory
I figure that gives them a year's vacation,
So boy oh boy, I gotta lotta vacations
       to live in a single life!
Maybe I'll give a few out to you
       my friends and readers.
Maybe if we all realize we should be
       all making up for the wasted lives
(So many now in the history of humans
       each of us would have to live a million lives
       to make up for all their lost vacations)
We can get back in touch with the time
       we were less like ants
And more like eagles soaring
       over the wilderness realms of the Earth.

"Your Poetry's No Good Because It Tries to Convey a Message"

Tell it to Jews hanging from meathooks,
Tell it to Wilfred Owen's exploded face,
Tell it to James Wright's cancerous cut-out tongue,
Tell it to Victor Jara's hands chopped off
      in Santiago Stadium,
Tell it to all the ears, breasts, cocks and balls
      cut off in every war,
Tell it to all the beautiful eyes
      gouged out in every war,
Tell it to the pyramid of human skulls
      that never stops growing,
Tell it to the decapitated head held up
      to gape twitching corpse jeering crowd,
Tell it to the fact we're all in Auschwitz because
      any second every city can become Holocaust,
Tell it to Hetch Hetchy, tell it to Glen Canyon,
      tell it to Wounded Knee and the Buffalo,
Tell it to the aluminum fibers in your brain
      and the cancer in your food and water
      which will eventually kill you,
Tell it to 100 trillion cigarets a year,
Tell it to 100 billion spent on war every minute,
Tell it to *Johnny Got His Gun*,
Tell it to the ashes of Neruda's library,
Tell it to 52 million children under 15
      working in factories in Southeast Asia,
Tell it to more people born in 2984
      than all the people ever born,
Tell it to the annihilated White Pine dominions
      of Wisconsin,
Tell it to the Sequoias still standing
      that were alive one thousand years
      before the Bible was written,
Tell it to all the unexperienced homosexual joy
      since Christianity came into power,
Tell it to the $100,000 it cost to kill
      each soldier in World War II,
Tell it to Henry Ford's factory in France
      that made tanks for the Third Reich,
Tell it to the sunrise, tell it to the rainbow,
      tell it to the flower made love to by the bee,
Tell it to the waterfall that never stops telling,
Tell it to the combers that never cease crashing,

Tell it to the reflection of stars
        in the rain-filled blackbear track,
Tell it to the canyons that echo
        the canyons that echo,
Tell it to birdsong, whalesong, wolfsong, cricketsong,
Tell it to the clouds as they float overhead,
        yell it to the lightning, bell it to the thunder,
        well it to the pouring rain, spell it
            on kindergarten blackboard,
        knell it to firefly cemetery dusk,
Tell it to tombstones who have forgotten their names,
Tell it to the shadow of your breathcloud
        on a winter day,
Tell it to mother harp seals
        while their babies are skinned alive,
Tell it to the naked black youth being hung
        by white lynchmob while they point and laugh,
Tell it to the geniuses who invent better and better
        methods of mass murder,
Tell it to the stockpiles of suicide pills
        to be dispensed in the event of apocalypse,
Tell it to the fact more women raped in America every year
        than poetry books sold every year,
Tell it to the statistics of ecocide, genocide, suicide,
Tell it to Kennedy's brainfragments
        quivering on the Dallas street,
Tell it to Sylvia Plath's head in the oven,
Tell it to Lorca while the soldier fires
        two bullets up his ass.
Tell it to Ishi on the L.A. Freeway during rush hour,
Tell it to Black Elk on Times Square at midnight
        on New Year's Eve,
Tell it to the Blue Whales and Redwoods
        murdered by harpoons and buzz-saws,
Tell it to the shadowgraphs in Hiroshima,
Tell it to the poets on Skid Row.

Winter Night Can Plant Return

Ten years after completing *Factory*
One snowy cold January night I return
    to my old alma mater—
Walk north along railroad tracks
    from Riverside Park to Estabrook Park,
Cutting across the snowy parkscape
    looking up at the Channel 6 Tower,
Over to the wooded slopes of the Milwaukee River
    and along the snowy trail,
Smelling the factory before actually seeing it,
    the acrid chemical taint,
Hearing the factory before actually seeing it,
    the weird metallic buzz,
Finally reaching where more rail tracks
    cross the river on an old wooden trestle,
Glimpsing through tree-branches at the slope's crest
    across the river through tree-branches
        beyond the far slope,
The gigantic can plant, all windows lit,
    thousandfold machineroar humming.
About to cross over
    I see a light flash from behind me
        and hear a train approach.
Backing into the brush, hiding behind an oak
    I spy the slow advance.
An old locomotive rumbles across,
    the bridge groans under its weight,
    the engineer peering ahead through falling snow,
The snow-hung trees illuminated, the swirls
    of snowgusts illuminated, then darkened
    as the lightbeam passes,
The darkened boxcars passing through falling snow,
    swaying gently side to side,
Ten boxcars full of coils of aluminum
    to be turned into millions of cans.
In the distance near the barbed-wire gate
    at the factory's rear
    a man swinging a lantern.
After uncoupling its load inside
    and switching tracks
        the engine returns alone.
After it's gone and its decrescendoing rumble is gone
    I cautiously cross the bridge
Pausing a moment halfway, gazing upstream—

the snow-covered ice, the tree-lined
dark park riverbanks, the wild night river scene
juxtaposed to Industry's Monument,
Closer yet I approach you O Factory
from which *Factory* originated!
Unsuspecting giant, blizzard-engulfed,
closer, closer—inside through your windows
once more I see the workers and the machines.
Funny, I could be a saboteur with a bomb,
or a spy or assassin.
Then I remember I already revealed
the top secret in *Factory*,
already blew up all factories with poetry.
This must be a deathbed mirage,
This trembling earth, this noise, these fumes,
the huge architecture is a dream.
Perhaps I lived here 5000 years ago
and time-warped into the future
to glimpse what was in store.
Perhaps my spaceship landed from another planet
and I emerged onto this scene.
Perhaps I died in the Wilderness and my spirit
returned here for some reason.
Secret rendezvous, secret rendezvous,
How could I have known how powerful you'd be to me?
The swirling snow, the intense cold, long after midnight,
no one else here,
No one on Earth knows I'm here
Standing smoking ceremonial smoke
on the deep snow tree-lined bluff,
looking over at and into Continental Can,
musing and being mused by these thoughts.
Why didn't the owners answer my letter
Requesting to give a performance of *Factory*
to the workers in the plant
when I sent them a complimentary copy?
Ten years after completing it I return
to find a sprawling two-story addition
plus another vast parking lot.
What good did my poem do after all?
The Factory I made disappear ten years ago
is twice as big!
Yet the very fact I stand here
smoking superb marijuana contemplation
confronting the actual monster
is a victory, as much a coup
as Sioux brave touching his enemy

and able to escape unharmed—
Only this "enemy" is working so hard
         it doesn't even know I'm here....
Snow covers my boots, icicles hang from my beard
         before I realize how long I've been standing
         motionless in the blizzard
                  looking in.
And then, retreating, beginning my long hike home,
         stopping every so often to look back,
         to see the receding vision
Till the canplant is lost from view,
Till only the noise and smell and trembling
         reach the plummeting rivercrest trail—
The epiphany, earthshaking
         as the earthshaking from factoryroar,
That it was when the locomotive vanished
         and its big noise vanished
         that the reality of the continuing noise
                  and earthquake tremble from canfactory
         rushed in on me,
Realization the ground-vibrating machineroar
         radiates outward in every direction
Like an earthquake that never stops.
How far out does that quake tremble?
What effect those tremors
         on our flesh, bones, brains?
As in diagrams projecting the impact
         of a nuclear bomb on a city
We should draw concentric circles from each factory
         to show the intensity, the reality
Each factory is a ground zero exploding
         its noise, products, pollution
                  in every direction,
The same as a bomb exploding
         but continuously for decades
                  and each of us blown up
         our whole life.

Why No "Poet Wanted"
In Want Ad Column

Those who regard it an affront you write poems
        and aren't working—
As if writing poems and being a poet were not valid work
        in our society,
As if Poetry has no value,
Especially when you write
        "Factories Are Boxcars Full of Jews,"
Especially when you invoke a marijuana blowjob religion,
Especially when you place Solitude Wilderness Vision Quest
        above all the Works of Man—
They want you to get a job you don't like
        and have to be working full-time
        so you can't write anymore.
They want you to confess
        your poetry is full of shit.
Somehow your writing
        threatens them.
Besides, Christ already said it all—
So don't bother trying to say
        something new that's true.
What are the words of a mere mortal
        next to the Son of God's?

Rebecca Falls Epiphany

We wish that beneficent beings from Outer Space
        would land on Earth and bring us the Vision we need
        to save us from destroying the world.
We wish a spaceship would come from Outer Space
        and transport us to its planet's Utopia
        where creatures exactly like us but enlightened
        or creatures very different from us but enlightened
            exist.
We wonder if some of the people we know
        aren't possibly from Outer Space,
Or complete strangers of unearthly beauty
        or great tender geniuses of love,
            poetry, music, dance, art—
        are they not emissaries from "out there"?
We wonder if possibly we are
        Outer Space Reconnaissance Consciousnesses
        programmed not to awake till now,
Cosmic Reconnaissance Renaissance Consciousnesses
        programmed not to awake till now.
What is my Mission on this planet?
What am I here for? What am I here for?
Ding! Ding! Ding! Ding! Ding!
Suddenly we realize WE ARE FROM OUTER SPACE!
        WE ARE CREATURES FROM OUTER SPACE!
        EARTH IS OUR PLANET IN OUTER SPACE!
We don't have to go in a spaceship from Earth to the moon
        and take Mescaline and look back at our Earth
        or walk in space after smoking
        millions of joints
        to realize we're in Outer Space!
We are just as much in Outer Space
        wherever we are on this Planet
        as we'd be on our moon
        or any moon in our solar system
        or any solar system in this galaxy
        or any galaxy in this universe
        or any universe in the pastpresentfuture!
We are as much creatures from Outer Space
        as lifeforms anywhere in this galaxy
        or any galaxy!
There's nowhere in the Universe
        that is more in Outer Space
        than we are!
We live *in* the Universe!

It's not "out there."
It's not just something we see in movies
        to eerie music.
We don't have to read science fiction
        to make love voluptuous cricketsinging nights
            under all the stars.
Thank you Mescaline and Marijuana for helping us perceive
        the mystical miraculousness of every day and every second
        and all living forms of life and every climate
        and geology, the seasons, the natures of
                seeing, hearing, smelling, tasting, touching,
                sleeping, dreaming, waking, laughing, loving,
                and the transformation of death!
Each of us should be as much an apparition as Bigfoot
        or LochNess Monster!
Each of us should be as much an apparition as the Being
        coming down the ramp of the spaceship
            from "out there."
How dear this Earth becomes then!
How sacred every wild place and creature
        that remains!
How insidious and lamentable the vast factory pollution
        and overpopulation disaster more disastrous
        than all the dead in every human war!
How clear it becomes to us then
        that no one should have to be a slave!
That everyone should be a creative genius of tender love
        and loving creator of music or poetry,
                painting or dance,
            endless continued gentle passionate creations
                of human mind!
Behold the lilies, they neither spin nor sew!
Think of the whales! They don't punch timeclocks!
        They don't need Christ or Buddha
            to be enlightened.
Everyone's life should be devoted to enlightenment!
Everyone should be free to receive Visions of Mescaline
        in absolute wilderness solitude!
Ah, I feel the key, for me, to perceiving, entertaining,
        and embodying Infinite Space and Eternal Time's
                Ultimate Implications
        is to be found in the deepest solitude I can find
                in the non-human Manifestation of Cosmos
        in that realm called Wilderness Reality.
What does Contemporary Poetry Scene in America
        have to do with this?
Do I live in America?

Do people who are dead continue to argue
        whether there is life after death?
This *is* Heaven!
I don't have to die
        to be Immortal!
I don't have to die
        to be in Eternity!
To feel in this flash of existence
        in the Antler form
        the unending Amaze!
O Poets are Emissaries from Outer Space
        descending their spaceship ramps
        and their visionary message to Earth
            shall be heard around the world!

from **CATCHING THE SUNRISE**

Raising My Hand

One of the first things we learn in school is
        if we know the answer to a question
We must raise our hand and be called on
        before we can speak.
How strange it seemed to me then,
        raising my hand to be called on,
How at first I just blurted out,
        but that was not permitted.

How often I knew the answer
And the teacher (knowing I knew)
Called on others I knew (and she knew)
        had it wrong!
How I'd stretch my arm
        as if it would break free
        and shoot through the roof
        like a rocket!
How I'd wave and groan and sigh,
Even hold up my aching arm
        with my other hand
Begging to be called on,
Please, *me*, I know the answer!
Almost leaping from my seat
        hoping to hear my name.

Twenty-nine now, alone in the wilds,
Seated on some rocky outcrop
        under all the stars,
I find myself raising my hand
        as I did in first grade
Mimicking the excitement
        and expectancy felt then.
No one calls on me
        but the wind.

Alan Watts Dying in His Sleep Elegy

> "What will it be like to go to sleep and never wake up?
> It makes me inevitably think of my birth, of waking up
> after having never gone to sleep!"

—*Beyond Theology* by Alan Watts

It was the new grass and Jeff couldn't wait.
I was just lighting a match when Jim and Carol came in the door
And the telephone rang with my mother telling me
    the newspaper said
Alan Watts died in his sleep.

After the first joint I sat in my antique dentist chair
    and taking the paddle I used in Quetico
        I paddled the air
    till I was in my canoe once more
        in the middle of Solitude Lake.
After the second joint Jim whispered
    you can go so far down in Mammoth Cave
        above the ceiling an underground river flows
    so big you can take boat trips on it
        and above the ceiling above the river
    lies an even more immense room of the cave,
And then Carol whispered a day's drive from Milwaukee
    are caves with sixty-foot underground waterfalls,
        and the way she told it
    we were there.
After the third joint Jeff and I became young animals
    wrestling and growling and biting each other
        to Beethoven mandolins
Till Jim appeared with a tub of hot water to soak our feet in
    while conducting the Vienna Choirboys
        accompanied by harp and the fourth joint
    laughing at the growing pool on the rug
Till Carol and I lugged the leaky tub to the porch
    and raced barefoot around the November block
        till back on the stoop, pants rolled to knees,
    we poured warm water over numb feet
        watching it waterfall down the steps
    and the rising steam
And before she knew it I'd locked her out
    and when she knocked
        the door opened a crack grinning
    "Who are you and what do you want?"

And after letting her in to Kodaly's songs for girls' chorus
    I crawled toward my writing room
        gibbering like a thirst-crazed man
And crawling back with another joint
    of the best grass since I smoked wilderness
        we smoked it
And then Chopin made me take the mirror shaped like a tombstone
    and walk toward Jim with it in front of my face
        so he saw his own face coming toward him
    and from behind his closed lips my voice—
        "How can I speak when I don't open my mouth?"
And then sitting down facing Jeff with his face
    I said—"What's your name? Can we be friends?"
And turning the mirror around on my lap
    I looked in my own face with surprise,
        gentleness, infatuation, lust,
    the slow blossoming of my smile,
And watching myself laugh
    I wished we all had mirrors on our laps
        and could have conversations with each other
    while watching ourselves speak,
And then Jeff put on Milhaud's "Scaramouche"
    and sitting facing each other
        balancing our feet
    we took turns dancing the beat
        on each other's soles
    passing back and forth laughs we hadn't laughed
        since wilderness smoked us,
And after the sixth wilderness I floated
    the beaverskull from Quetico in candlelight
    toward Carol's face
And accompanied by Jeff and Jim's shouts of "Popcorn! Popcorn!"
    I told Carol I believe each of us is living right now
        on millions of planets
    because if I were God I'd have made it that way,
And then I created popcorn
    with just enough butter
        and we washed it down with cold slugs of beer
And after the seventh day of creation
    Jeff brought in ten concert grands
        playing the William Tell Overture
And I stood on my head till I no longer could

Then danced with the mirror
      whirling in circles at top speed
            till my reflection and I collapsed
            in epilepsies of laughter
            and sprawled exhaustion my heart
            pounding harder than ever
            gazed up at the ceiling still spinning
            as the lights clicked on and off on and off
            on and off on and off on and off...

Alan Watts—*you'll never know you died.*

November 17, 1973

Put This In Your Pipe And Smoke It!

If the solar system were five miles long
      the sun would be a three-foot sphere
            and the Earth a pea a footballfield away!
If the Milky Way were ten miles long
      the solar system would be the size of a pinhead
            and the sun a millionth of an inch!
If the sun were the dot over an "i"
      the nearest star would be the dot over an "i"
            24 miles away!
A million Earths could easily fit in our sun
      yet some stars are so big
            six billion suns our size
                  could easily fit inside!

The size of my winking eye compared to the sun!

Pretending to Be Dead

How many boys who loved playing army,
Who loved pretending to be shot
          tumbling down summer hills,
Who loved pretending to be dead
          as their bestfriend checked to make sure,
Or who loved pretending to deliver
          their last-words soliloquy
          wincing in imagined pain
          or lost and dreamy,
Find themselves years later
          trapped on the battlefield
Hearing the voices of enemy soldiers
Searching for corpses to mutilate
          or wounded to torture to death?

What man remembers those idyllic
          boyhood days then
As he lies still as possible
Trying not even to breathe,
          hoping beyond hope
          the enemy will pass him by,
Knowing if he's discovered
          they'll cut off his cock and balls
          and stuff them in his screaming mouth
And then, before cutting off his head,
          disembowel him before his eyes?

Ah, thousands of boys and men
          have met this end,
Millions perhaps by now,
          so many people
          so many wars.
Do they go to a special heaven
          set aside for
          all who die like this?
Restored to the bodies they had,
The memory erased of that insane end
          to the story of their lives?

Do they still get a chance
          to play army with joy
And pretend to be shot
          and pretend to die
After they meet this end?

Do they still get to thrill
          in pretending to be dead
          after they die?
After this hideous inhuman end
          will they laugh and wrestle
          their bestfriend again?

Bringing Zeus to His Knees

In the drained reflecting pool in the small park
        facing San Francisco City Hall during
        the June 12, 1982 Nuclear Disarmament Rally
A barechested boy lying on his back, arms behind
        his head, eyes closed,
        sunbasking.
As speaker after speaker gives
        inspiring talk
And the crowd roars and applauds,
        all faces turned toward the stage,
The boy lies there—where last week seagulls floated
        on turquoise ripples.
Does he hear the great pleas for peace?
Or is he dozing?
Perhaps he was listening before
        behind his closed eyes
        his dreamlovegirl or boy appeared
        and glowed and gleamed.
How many loving eyes caress this Vision
        that does not see them?
How many strolling from the rapt crowd
        to rest their ears from the anti-war fervor
        they so much agree with
        and which inspires so many of their poems,
Come upon this Vision and are overcome
        with the dazzling sight of naked boyhood
        armpits and chest and belly and face
        that would bring Zeus to his knees—
I stare uncaring if any see me.
The boy does not open his eyes.
He could be on a hilly grassy meadow
        or inflatable raft in a blue pool
        or on his bed taking a summer nap.
I stare so long so lovingly I'm surprised
        the whole crowd doesn't turn
        to watch me staring and join
        in a staring silent circle
        around this apparition
        fallen from heaven.
The beautiful halfnaked sleeping boy Vision
        says more to me against war,
        against nuclear power, arms race,
        nationalism, imperialism, slavery,
        than all the fiery diatribes put together.

Suddenly I see the boy burn alive,
      his flesh afire writhing screaming pyre,
And the crowd melting flaming agonied forms
      from World War III's imagined holocaust reality,
And then I see him as before
      and see myself kneeling
      by his side
      as before a manger
Lavishing with ecstatic love
      my boylove dream.

Whitmansexual

Whitman was a boysexual, a girlsexual,
      a womansexual, a mansexual,
A grasssexual, a treesexual,
      a skysexual, an earthsexual.
Whitman was an oceansexual, a mountainsexual,
      a cloudsexual, a prairiesexual,
A birdsongsexual, a lilacsmellsexual,
      a gallopinghorsesexual.
Whitman was a darknesssexual, a sleepersexual,
      a sunrisesexual, a MilkyWaysexual,
A gentlebreezesexual, an openroadsexual,
      a wildernesssexual, a democracysexual,
A drumtapssexual, a crossingbrooklynferrysexual,
      a sands-at-seventy-sexual.
Whitman was a farewell-my-fancy-sexual,
      a luckier-than-was-thought-sexual,
A deathsexual, a corpsewatchsexual,
      a compostsexual, a poets-to-come-sexual,
A miracle-sexual, an immortalitysexual,
      a cosmos-sexual, a waiting-for-you-sexual.

Ejaculation

Every Universe is an ejaculation!
Every sun is an ejaculation!
Every Earth is an ejaculation!
Every being is an ejaculation!
Women ejaculate babies!
Girls ejaculate breasts!
Boys are ejaculations that ejaculate!
Men ejaculate six million ejaculations per orgasm!
Everyone alive ejaculates their corpse!
Everything we eat is an ejaculation!
Fruit and vegetables are ejaculations!
Trees are ejaculations—they burst up and collapse
            in a speeded-up movie of time!
Every leaf is an ejaculation!
The Earth ejaculates wildflowers every spring!
The sea is a continual ejaculation!
Look at the youth surfboarding the orgasms!
Every cloud is an ejaculation!
Every lightning is an ejaculation!
Every drop of rain or snow is an ejaculation!
Every sunrise is an ejaculation!
Every waterfall is an ejaculation!
Every meteor is an ejaculation!
Every mountain is an ejaculation!
Every grain of sand is an ejaculation!
Every second that passes is an ejaculation!
This Universe has been ejaculating 100 billion years!
Scientists listen by radio telescope
            to the Big Bang's orgasmcry!
Every word spurts from our mouth!
Every book, symphony, statue, painting, film,
            house, car, plane, ship, train
            ejaculates from some brain!
Every exclamation point is an ejaculation!
Every inhalation and exhalation
            is an ejaculation!
Every shit is an ejaculation!
Every spaceship is an ejaculation!
Every nation is an ejaculation!
Every religion is an ejaculation!
Every Bible is an ejaculation!
Every Savior is an ejaculation!
I calculate ejaculate ululates through All!
Show me anything that's not an ejaculation!

Lip-Licking Deer Shitting Meditation

When you become such good friends with black-tailed deer
  that live in the black oak forest
    Sierra Foothills
That 20 feet away they graze contemplating you
  as you sit on a stump in silence
    admiring them
And they think nothing of shitting in front of you
  looking over their shoulders
    across their backs and rear-ends
  their black tails lifted
As the perfectly-shaped same-size brown pellets fountain out
  in a delicate continuous fountain,
And when they gaze at you
  with their big black eyes
    while they shit
And suddenly their long pink tongues curl out
  and they're licking their lips,
Licking their lips while shitting
  and looking over at you
    with their deep shy eyes,
Isn't it proper etiquette to lick your lips back,
  to think nothing of pissing in front of them,
    showing off your cock
  and the long arc of urine
    saved up for them
  knowing they like
    its salty savor
  like salad dressing
    on their grass and mushrooms,
Isn't it proper etiquette you should look at them
  curious playful friendly
    and lick your lips in return?

Bedrock Mortar Full Moon Illumination

Seeing the reflection of the full moon
    in the rainfilled bedrock mortar holes
        where earliest California Indians
        ground acorns with circular grinding stones
And sensing how the full moon
    is like a mortar stone in the sky,
And then seeing the image of my face
        looking up at me from the moonlit surface
            and sensing my own evanescence,
        how my face is like an acorn
            time grinds to fine dust,
And thinking thousands of years
        Indians ground acorns here
Singing their acorn songs
        gossiping and laughing
            or silent and musing
        listening to the pleasing sound
            of mortar stones grinding acorns
Or after a big storm
        gazing in the rainfilled holes
            at their reflections
        or seeing the full moon mirrored
Or deer hot from play
        dipping shy twilight muzzles
            in the cool pools
As blue oak and black oak
        ponderosa pine and digger pine
            incense cedar and manzanita
        grew and died in continuous
            ever-changing spots
        around the site.
Yet just as surely years from now
        faces staring here
After scooping out fallen leaves
        and feeling with future fingers
            the wet smooth tapering holes
        in the mossy lichen-covered rock
            contemplating themselves
        looking up at themselves
            contemplating these same thoughts
        will vanish,
While century after century the full moon
        continues to stare down
            and see its face

unseen by anyone in the forest
Reflected in the rainfilled mortar holes
    from long ago.

Childfoot Visitation

One night traveling a Green Tortoise bus
    San Francisco to Seattle,
The rear of the bus converted to pads for sleeping,
Sleeping on my back as we plunged through pouring rain,
    the other weary passengers sleeping,
Suddenly something moving in my beard and under my nose
    woke me up—
Opening my eyes in the darkness
    I saw in the flickering headlight patterns
    of passing cars
The small foot of the little girl sleeping
    beside her mother.
Cleansmelling childfoot flower stretching beneath my nose
    as she changed position in her dream.
Gently pushing it away, careful not to wake her,
    I drifted off to sleep
Thinking how many men who never had a child
    are visited by a childhood foot
    slowly sliding through their beards
    opening their eyes to
    its perfect shape in the twilight?
Suddenly out of Eternity coming to me
    white and pink and smelling good,
For the first time in my life
    a little girl's naked foot
    woke me up.

Catching the Sunrise

When I see the first light
        touch treetops on the far shore
I launch my canoe without a sound
        and float into perfect calm.
Not till the lakefloor disappears
        do I dip my paddle
And begin without a sound
        for the other side.
Not a drip or a ripple
        I go so slow.
When I reach the center of the lake
        the sun is up enough
        the far shore glows.
Soon I'm paddling in sunlight,
        mist rises in wraiths.
On seeing the bottom
        as I near the other side
I stop paddling and glide,
        not a breath of wind.
Bird sings. Fish jumps.
Looking back where I came from
        I can see the trees at my camp
        begin to be touched by the sun.

What the God Says Through Me

You won't hear my poems at the poetry reading.
You won't hear my poems over the radio.
If you want what the God says through me
Come alone with me into Quetico
        and we'll canoe across lake after lake
        where there are no roads or houses
To a perfect lake with a perfect island
Where you and I will pitch our camp
        and catch fish for twilight supper.

Sitting around the fire at night
Ask me to read something I wrote
For this is the place to hear me,
More stars overhead than you ever saw,
        no other light in the woods for miles,
        no other sound but the loon
And the night wilderness smells of September.
This is the place to hear my voice
        if you want what the God says through me.

To All Wilderness Views

Offering the View the joint,
Offering the joint the View—
        so the View can be high too,
But the View is already high,
        the View of Views.
Feasting my eyes on the View
        a zen of horizons dawns.
Do I agree with the View?
Does the View agree with me?
What are my views compared to its views?

Reviewing my life in view of the View,
I see what my prospect is from the prospect.
A prospector of prospects, my outlook is
        my vantage point, my perspective is
        my overview.
Having a Viewpoint helps in having
        a point of view—
Taking in the View,
The View takes you in too.
You're in the View and the View's in you.

After All Is Said and Done

I want to lie down in dappled leaf-shade,
In quivering shadows of quivering leaves—
        be they oak, be they maple,
        be they elm or birch,
I want to rest in the play of shadows
        over my reclining form,
The massage of shadows
        which consoles me in its way,
Restores for me
        with whatever restoration
Flickering shadows of leaves afford—
        be they willow or aspen,
        be they poplar or beech,
I want to be caressed by shadows
        of wavering leaves,
Soothed off to sleep
        feeling the gentle breeze,
Looking up at the rustling
        sun-drenched crown—
Be it basswood, be it chestnut,
Be it walnut or hickory,
        after all is said,
        after all is done,
This is the way
I would die.

Campfire Talk

Birds don't need opinions
    because they have pinions,
What is the opinion of the piñon pine
    on whether Christianity is
    for or against homosexuality?
A flower doesn't need a savior
    to be able to bloom.
A waterfall doesn't need a guru
    in order to gush.
A caterpillar doesn't need a Bible
    to become a butterfly.
A lake doesn't need a Ph.D.
    to become a cloud.
A rainbow doesn't need a fresh coat of paint
    every year.
Worms don't need to study existentialism
    to exist.
Mountains don't need to kneel
    and ask forgiveness for their sins.
Capitalism and Communism mean nothing
    to every tree that alchemizes light.
No whale will ever know who Christ is.
No chipmunk will ever follow Buddha.
No owl gives a hoot about Mohammed.
No grizzly will ever consult a priest.
No seagull will ever become a Mormon.
No dolphin has to learn computers
    if it wants to get along
    in the modern world.
No sparrow needs insurance.
No gorilla needs a God.

Atheist Conches

Are there conches that don't believe
      after they die they echo the sea?
That try to prove to other conches
      the foolishness of believing after they die
        they will echo the sea?
Spend their lives trying to persuade them
      there is no air or beach,
        only the sea,
      and when you die that's it,
        there's no echo?

Necropolis In Metropolis

Joggers among colossal obelisks,
Birdwatchers with binoculars poised before
            miniature parthenon mausoleums,
Highschool sweethearts showing each other
            poignant inscriptions they found.
Their genitals alive, healthy, titillated
            by existence daily,
While underground thousands of dead genitals,
            shrunken, foul-smelling, rotting or already dust,
            no scraps of penis or vagina flesh
            on the silent motionless skeleton.
Names on tombstones are hot to the touch
            in the spring sun.
Some of the names on these stones
Have existed longer
Than the person who lived and died
            and is buried beneath.
19-year-old killed at Gettysburg—
            "After long agony, rapture and bliss,
            Right was the path leading to this."
All the graves continually bathed
            by nearby freeway roar.
Millard Fillmore's grave, first President's grave
            I visited in my life.
"The nourishment is palatable," I repeat his last words
            to his final resting place.
The lifespan of tombstones exists.
No relatives and close friends gather round
            a tombstone's deathbed.
A tombstone's last words are the wind.
Discover tombstone of a man from Buffalo
            who it says died in Milwaukee
            but his body was shipped back to Buffalo
            to be buried here.
Watch a young blindman led by a nun
            kneeling and brailling a name
            on a tilting weathered stone.

                         Forest Lawn Cemetery
                         Buffalo, New York

Babyteeth Necklace

Children should save their babyteeth—
Each one when it falls out
      could be put in a special box
         until all twenty
      could be carefully strung
         on a necklace
So that when they reach puberty
      the boy or girl they become
         could wear
      the garland of their milkteeth,
And so the old man or old woman they become
      could finger the rosary
         of their childhood teeth
And be buried wearing them or bequeath
      their babyteeth to be worn
         as amulets by their grandchildren
      before they're old enough to wear their own.

One Breath

One of your breaths contains
        all the air
                a Mayfly breathes
        in its life.

All the Breaths

All the breaths all the people
        who ever lived or are alive now
                breathe in their life put together
        could fit in a space
            as big as
        Lake Michigan,
Whereas an ant's total breaths in its life
        would fill a space
            the size of
        your body,
And a human breathes
        a space of air in its life
            the size of
        the Empire State Building,
And a Blue Whale breathes a volume
        so large in its life
            you could go backpacking in it
        for a month
            and see no one.

Marijuana Saved My Life

Heard from my grandmother
An old Bible in her attic told
In the part reserved for family histories
How one of my ancestors came over on the Mayflower—
      John Howland, a 13-year-old boy
Who was swept overboard in a storm.
Someone threw a rope over the side into the dark
      and miraculously he caught it
      and was hauled back in,
"And if he hadn't caught that rope,
      you wouldn't be here now."
Thirty years later I realize
Way back then rope was hemp
      and so:
Marijuana saved my life!

Smuggling the Dust of Immortals

Flying back from Europe to Milwaukee
    peering down at the Pyrenees
        where the antler'd dancer
        dances on the ceiling of a cave,
Seeing the Atlantic spread before me,
    thinking back to Rome
        to my visit to the Protestant Cemetery,
    my afternoon alone there
        with the graves of Shelley and Keats,
Speaking poems by them by heart
    to their final resting place,
        and taking a pinch of soil
    from each grave
        in a plastic bag,
Little suspecting when I landed in New York
    the customs inspector would find it,
        open it, sniff the contents,
        eye me suspiciously: "What's this?"
Gravesoil from Keats and Shelley's graves."
    "Who are they?"

Bubble-Boggled

Under the Locust Street Bridge at midnight
    in the middle of the frozen Milwaukee River
        alone with a bottle of wine,
    the starry nightsky twinkling on either side,
Getting on my knees, kneeling on the snow,
    looking where the wind blew the snow away
        exposing the ice like a window,
    a window I can see through,
A black window I can look through
    putting my face to the surface
        to oggle and be boggled
    by bubbles frozen
        at different levels
    in different shapes and sizes,
        white in color,
    suspended, motionless,
And thinking the moment these bubbles froze
    wondering if anyone ever saw
        the moment a bubble froze,
    the moment an air globule
        gurgling and burbling
    on its upward rush
        caught solid in icy hold.
What goes on in a frozen bubble?
Does a frozen bubble believe
    it will still be a frozen bubble
        after it melts?
Thought of when they melt,
    rising at last, freed....
Thought of people who drowned
    whose last bubble breaths
        froze midway,
    frozen last words waiting for spring
        and those who listen for them....
Thought of bubbles lasting millions of years
    in icecaps....
Thought of bubbles trapped in lava,
    dark airpockets in rock aeons....
Thought of bubbles rising from canoe paddles
    unstuck from swamp muck....
Bubbles in puddles created and destroyed
    by falling rain....
Bubbles with rainbows quivering
    at the base of waterfalls....

Hippopotamus fartbubbles big as hulahoops,
      frogfartbubbles small as a needle's eye....
Thought of underwater spiders who struggle bubbles of air
      to their underwater webs to breathe from....
Thought of bubbles of thought in cartoons....
Thought of bubbles sparkling up bottles
      stared at by drunks for centuries....
Thought of carpenter observing bubble in his level
      as he adjusts the angle of a beam....
Thought of whales in love caressing each other
      with bubbles....
Thought of girls bobbling their baubles
      goggled by bubble-blowing boys....
Thought of babyblubbering hushed by motherbreast,
      bubble of milk on sleeping lips....
Thought of Imagination Bubble-wand dipped in solution
      strewing bubble flotillas on the breeze,
          different sizes and shapes of poems
    at different levels
        rising and frozen as they rise,
      mind-bubbles caught for a moment
        observed suspended in time
     floating, reflecting....
Thought how I'm only a bubble
     rising from birth to death
        changing my shape
     from child to man as I rise....
Thought of the Earth as a bubble,
     the Sun as a bubble,
        the Galaxies bubbles
    sparkling, flowing, bursting
        on the black river of space,
    on the black river of time....
Thought of the sound of a bubble's pop....
Thought how many bubbles there have been....
Everpresent evanescent effervescence.
Mind-boggled by bubbles
     I gaze with awe
        through black window ice
Realizing bubbles frozen in ice
     as if I never saw them before,
        as if I never knew
     they existed,
Bubbles frozen in ice,
How I bent to look at them,
How I crouched on my hands and knees
     on the snow

And put my face to the ice
     and peered down at them
          motionless, suspended,
    a long time
Milwaukee River New Year's Eve 1984.

Looking Through Baby Footprints

Two-inch baby footprints on
     completely frosted window
          of second floor lobby
     Performing Arts Center downtown Milwaukee
          after hearing Bruckner Mass #2—
Perfect baby footprints in frost
     you could look through and see
          cars going by
     in subzero January night.
Imagine expression babyface when mother
     pressed tiny feet on ice-cold glass—
To calm her baby from crying or play a game?
Watch dowagers in furs
     helped by chauffeurs
          into parked limousines
     through baby footprint impressions
          while respectable concertgoers
     emerge into lobby
          observing me in my bum-clothes.

Eye to Eye

Gazing through
    my reflection
        to see
a trout's eye
    looking up at me
        through where
the reflection
    of my eye is
        on the water.

A Second Before It Bursts

Seeing my reflection on a river
    and seeing a bubble float into my reflection
        the bubble also reflecting me,
So I see the reflection of my face in a bubble
    in the reflection of my face
        on the river,
While below on the bottom
    the shadow of the bubble passes over
        golden fallen sunken leaves
So it looks like inside my face is a river bottom
    of golden fallen sunken leaves
        with the shadow of a bubble passing over
    while on the surface
My reflected face with a bubble moving in it
    also reflecting me
        and me thinking
It will burst any second
    just before it
        bursts. . . .

Paleolithic Consciousness
Orbited by TVs

How close the closest TV to me?
My head seen from above
    and then x-ray vision over
        roofs of Milwaukee
    showing turned-on TVs
    with people glued to them—
Thousands and thousands in a one-mile radius from my head,
    dozens of channels, dozens of voices and plots,
        endless commercials, endless actors
    and actresses in costumes gesticulating,
        endless images flashing on gazers' eyes,
While in the center—my poet head,
    my meditating poetry brain
        in silence at midnight
    in candlelight in my attic
        listening
    to the foghorn and the rain....

Unbrainwash Work Ethic!

Looking for a job is a job in itself
        to be worked at every day
        seven days a week!
If people learn you aren't working
        and aren't looking for work
        they think you aren't doing anything.
In not doing anything you cease
        to *be* anything.

                    *

A factoryworker fired from his job
        returns and shoots his boss.
Mobs protesting lack of jobs
        tear down the wrought-iron fence
        surrounding the governor's mansion.
Thousands of steelworkers demonstrate against
        impending overhaul of their plant
        that threatens to lay off thousands.
Out-of-work poor march on Washington
        demanding Congress create more jobs.
Some states will pay through taxes
        half the cost of building a factory
        to lure industrialists to build it in their state.
Every 1% increase in the U.S. Unemployment Rate
        brings one million more suicides,
        two million more heart-attacks,
        three million more alcoholics,
        four million more mental cases.
Some who win million dollar lotteries
        keep working their old job anyway.
Not working you feel worthless.
You go to the checkout counter and think
        at least the cashier has a job.

                    *

"Billions are to be made yearly
        by launching factories into space
To mine ore from the asteroid belt
        for medicine to fight cancer,
        creating new jobs all the way!
Companies putting payloads in space
        should be encouraged to move decisively.
All think-tanks agree—by the end of the century
        orbiting factories will surely

be established in space."

*

Frank Lloyd Wright once said:
"I will design a factory so beautiful
      it will be as inspiring a place to work in
          as any cathedral ever was to worship in."

*

"Now for a tour of a concentration camp,
      it's educational.
No advance registration is required.
Just be sure to wear comfortable walking shoes.
Children under 14 must be accompanied by an adult.
First, the gas shower rooms. Look through
      the thick glass windows. See
      the naked subhumans being processed.
Yes, they do put up a struggle and look in agony
      but experts assure us it's involuntary
      muscle action.
It's actually a quite pleasant death: note
      how every man and boy's corpse
      has an erection
And every female's nipples
      are erect.
Next, a favorite stop, the crematorium.
Then, on to the unburied mass-graves
      where visitors can sample decaying cadavers.
Everyone leaves with a pried-out tooth
      for a souvenir."

*

They want me to cut my long hair and beard
      wear a suit and tie
      and go in and out of skyscrapers
          with a briefcase.
They want me back in the factory
      sweating pathetic disillusioned
          repudiating my *Factory* poem.
They want me cleaning toilets
      of capitalist entrepreneurs younger than me.
They want me delivering supermarket circulars
      with bums who can't read or write.
They want me on my knees begging God
      for forgiveness for giving blowjobs
          devoutly and fervently.
They want me institutionalized
      under psychiatric care.

They know what drugs are best for me.
They want me to salute the flag
          with tears in my eyes.
They want me to say 1984
          was nothing like the book.
They want me to write factories are so great
          we should beg to work in them
                    for free.
They tell me I can still write poetry
          and have a full-time factory
                    or computer job,
That I can write on my time off
          as a hobby.
Better I write poetry full-time
          and have a job on the side,
Better writing poetry full-time my job
          and do no other work at all,
Better not to think of poetry
          as a job, as work,
But play, divine play,
          a joy like a singing bird
                    or leaping dolphin.
As Nietzsche said—"Live
          as though the day were here."

                    *

When asked "What do you do?"
          and you say—"I'm a poet,"
People always respond—"But what do you *really* do?"
Whereas if you say—"I'm a moviestar, rockstar, priest,
          policeman, businessman,"
No one would respond—"What do you *really* do?"
When asked "What do you do?"
And the person says—"I'm a factoryworker,"
          we should respond—"But what do you *really* do?'
Or the person says—"I'm a stockbroker, corporate head, banker,"
          we should say—"What do you *really* do?"
Not till people don't respond—"What do you *really* do?"
          when you tell them you're a poet
          is there any hope for America!

                    *

I gave up a career as a filmmaker,
          thinking there was more money in poetry.
Now I'm a self-employed poet who has laid himself off
          and wants to collect unemployment.
The problem is not so much a throwaway can,
          but a throwaway life, throwaway society,

                    throwaway planet.
Unbrainwash work ethic!
High unemployment exists—
            instead of cutting work hours,
                work week, work life,
            and establishing job sharing—
Because high unemployment keeps people in line:
"When jobs are scarce they can be kept
            for the most hard-working and submissive.
Trouble-makers, radicals, poets and deadbeats—
            they can remain without work—
They've only themselves to blame,
There's no room for wise guys anymore."

                    *

Why turn prisons into factories
            when factories are already prisons,
When Western Civilization already imprisoned
            in work-ethic work-life mindset?
Why not prosperity via poetry
            rather than industry?
Why not work less earn more,
            work less live more,
            work less love more?
Why have an ever-expanding economy
            when you can have an ever-expanding wilderness?
According to Ecotopia Consultant Antler
What we're experiencing is good news:
            Employment is down and Freedom is up.
Good news: Factories continue to close
            and workers can return to school
            to learn whatever they want for free!
Tomorrow's jobs and workers of tomorrow
            are a thing of the past!
After believing for centuries
            that time is money
And that nothing is worth more
            than selling one's time,
It dawns on us
            the more people work
                and the harder they work
            the more tired they are,
                the less time they have to think,
            to work for social change,
                for ecology and peace.
But maybe the reason we work so hard
            is so we don't have time to think,
            to think about our death and dying.

The freer people are, the more they think,
      the more mortality dawns on them,
          the more they realize
      their whole lives could be spent
          meditating on the ripples
   from the stone of their brief existence
          thrown into the still lake.

                *

Are we dogs muzzled with jagged tincans
      our front legs tied behind our backs,
Dragged to streetmarkets to be butchered alive
      and eaten?
Or are we daydreaming on our pig-belly cutting job
      our chain mail glove making it easier
          to grip the slippery bellies
      while we slit them
Thinking of the cabin we'll build up North
      after we retire?

                *

Faulkner said work is the only thing we can do
      8 hours a day
Because we can't eat, drink or make love that long.
Wrong! We can eat, drink and make love
      and read and think and go for long walks
      and tinker some art out of our souls
      48 hours a day!
As Lafargue said—"Work is the mere condiment
      to the pleasures of idleness."
As Oscar Wilde said—"Work is for those who have nothing
      better to do."
As Mark Twain said—"I don't like work
      even when the other fellow does it."
Reagan in his Inaugural Address said—
      "It's time to reawaken the Industrial Giant.
Putting America back to work means
      putting *all* America back to work."
I say put America back to play.
I say put America back to fun.
I say put America back to enlightenment.
I say put America back to Wilderness.
I say put America back to Love.
Rather than revitalize America's industrial base,
      revitalize America's poetry base,
      vision base, love base.
Heavy poetry more than heavy industry!

Hearing the Echo

Spend a rainforest on a hamburger.
Spend an ozonelayer on a refrigerator.
Spend a mountainrange to buy an electric range.
Spend a thousand-year-old tree on disposable
        chopsticks.
Spend a generation of young men in World War I
        so World War II won't happen.
Buy a tuna sandwich with a slaughtered dolphin.
Buy an airconditioner with a runaway Greenhouse Effect.
Spend the Great Lakes to possess a Jacuzzi.
Spend the best years of a humanbeing's life in a factory
        as a factoryworker praising your job
            while your great-great grandfather's
        boyorgasmcries wait for you
            to hear the echo of their echo.
Purchase furcoats with deathcries
        of endangered species.
Spend the suspended sentences of execution
        to deathrow inmates
            on exciting new advertising
        for skyrocketing cigaret sales
            in Third World countries.
Spend the astonished look of delight in a baby's eyes
        on car-bombs that disfigure
            the unsuspecting victim.
Spend the vows of lifelong love
        made by a boy and girl
            on new improved body bags
        for our dead soldiers
            that are guaranteed
        not to leak or burst.

Me a Screaming Eco-Meemie?

It's not my workpoems that are excessive
       but acid rain smokestacks that are excessive.
It's not my workmeditations that are repetitive
       but assemblylines that are repetitive.
It's not my factorypoems that are overworked
       but the eight-hour workday
            five-day workweek
     three-week vacation
          retirement at 65
     that's overworked,
When we could have a four-hour workday
       four-day workweek
           four-month vacation
     and retirement at 30.
It's not my workmusings that are overdone
       but prayers to a Homophobic God
           repeated over and over
       24 hours a day
           the last 4000 years
     that are overdone.
It's the very existence of clocks and timeclocks
       that's excessive.
It's the multinational monopolies that are too much.
It's the ecocide executives that are rabid radicals.
It's the arms race that's an extremist.
The work-ethic itself is excessive.
It's ranting and hollering more than me.
It's more didactic than me.
Money is more preachy than me.
Money is more strident than me.
Money is saying the same thing over and over.
Money keeps harping on and on.
Money keeps hammering away at the same point.
Money beats me over the head with its message.
Money exhausts the subject.
Money is belaboring the obvious.
Money is overdoing it.
Money is overkill.
Was Monet excessive to paint so many waterlilies?
Rodin excessive to sculpt so many nudes?
It's not my *Factory* that's a tirade
       but America's factories
           that are a tirade.
It's not me that has an ax to grind

but the logging industry
      that has an ax to grind.
Rather than putting your nose to the grindstone,
      put your nose to the marijuana stone.
Rather than putting your nose to the grindstone
      put your nose to the rosettastones of roses.
It's 50,000 nuclearbombs that are subversive
      not 50,000 voluptuous cunnilinguspoems.
It's not that my erotic poems are overblown
      but that teenage boys are underblown.
It's not my *ReWorking Work* that's long-winded
      but plutonium that's long-winded.
It's eight H-bombs created every day
      that don't know when to stop.
Every skyscraper is a screaming meemie!
Every factory every factorywhistle is a screaming meemie!
Every oilspill toxic waste dump is a screaming meemie!
Every Amazon chainsaw is a screaming meemie!
Every hole in the ozone layer the size of Texas
      is a screaming meemie!
Every nuclearpowerplant meltdown is a screaming meemie!
Every ever-increasing defense budget a screaming meemie!
Every pile-driver jackhammer drill-press drill-sergeant
      a screaming meemie!
Every motorboat lawnmower snowmobile a screaming meemie!
Every billboard TV commercial blaring boombox a screaming meemie!
Every hysterical evangelist a screaming meemie!
Every Bible with rabies a screaming meemie!
Every torture massacre assassination prison insane asylum
      slaughterhouse a screaming meemie!
Every rushhour trafficjam a screaming meemie!
Every overpopulation baby a screaming meemie!
Every husband and wife at each other's throats
      screaming meemies!
Every cashregister a screaming meemie!
Every sportscaster screaming homerun or touchdown
      a screaming meemie!
Every stadium full of screaming fans a screaming meemie!
Every city bursting into mushroomcloud a screaming meemie!

Me a screaming eco-meemie?
Your guess is as good as mine.

"Your Poetry's No Good Because It's Too Easy To Understand"

Tell it to nuclear bombs carried in suitcases
    by international terrorists.
Tell it to the prison being built
    across the street from Walt Whitman's house.
Tell it to moles that can run
    through their underground tunnels
        faster than racehorses gallop.
Tell it to 15,000 in Rio de Janeiro
    who applied for 260 streetsweeper jobs
        that paid $4 a day—
    many were university graduates and teachers
        who went hungry or sold their blood
    to pay the $1 application fee.
Tell it to more Barbie Dolls ever made
    than populations of London, Tokyo, Paris,
        New York and Los Angeles combined.
Tell it to Harvey Milk's exploded face.
Tell it to power shovels 10 stories high
    gouging 10 tons of earth in a single bite.
Tell it to eyeballs melting down the melting cheeks
    of the brain-melting skull
        which melts too.
Tell it to testicles of dying soldiers cut off
    and placed where their gouged-out eyes were.
Tell it to the fingers of the man who jumped off the dam
    which were completely worn away
        by trying to clutch his way up
    because he changed his mind.
Tell it to enough solid waste excreted by America every day
    to fill the Superdome from floor to ceiling 100 times.
Tell it to 100 Milwaukees added to the Earth every year.
Tell it to one million more cars every day.
Tell it to the fact more women raped in America every year
    than poetry books sold every year.
Tell it to the rainforest, the rainforest.
Tell it to the condor, the condor.
Tell it to unnamed waterfalls falling over
    overhanging cliffs.
Tell it to rippling patterns of light
    reflected from the creek
        on undersides of leaves and ferns.
Tell it to the hand impressions in Lascaux and Altamira.
Tell it to the hand impression I made in third grade

pressing my palm in plaster-of-paris pie plate.
Tell it to the fawn's yawn in the twilight thicket.
Tell it to the naked boy statue gently unearthed.
Tell it to schoolboy heroworship reminiscence.
Tell it to velvet perineums
    that've never been stroked by a feather.
Tell it to the honeysuckle in full-blow.
Tell it to the Sun that doesn't have to put postage on its rays
    to send them out.
Tell it to Alexander Dumas's mother who forced him to wear
    iron shoes as a child because he always walked on tiptoe
        as if about to soar away.
Tell it to Céline who wrote—"To write for posterity
    is to declaim to an audience of maggots."
Tell it to the 10 tons of termites that exist per person
    on Earth.
Tell it to the number of people who starve to death per year
    equal to 2000 *Titanic*s sinking every day
        with no survivors.
Tell it to workers in Haiti who screw caps on toothpastetubes
    for 7 cents an hour.
Tell it to Calcutta foundry workers who work 10 hours a day
    for a dollar making sewercovers for American streets.
Tell it to exegetes who maintain
    the more difficult a poem is to understand
        the better it is.
Tell it to the backpacker hearing commercials
    coming from his mouth
        because fillings in his teeth
    picked up radio waves.
Tell it to skyscrapers which have to take seasickness pills
    in strong winds.
Tell it to want ad sections of newspapers
    blowing down midnight downtown streets.
Tell it to want ad sections from 100 years ago
    yellowing in attics or between old house walls.
Tell it to babies born with erections.
Tell it to the deathturd that squeezes from your corpse.
Tell it to Sequoias that died before you were born
    and are still standing
        and will still be standing
    after you're dead.
Tell it to the tipped-over tree whose root-system
    has been clutching a boulder
        longer than you've been alive.
Tell it to the moose staring at its reflection in the lake.
Tell it to lions who only spend four hours a day on their feet,

the other twenty hours lounging around.
Tell it to the cement mixer driver
    who had to go inside his cement mixer
        with a jackhammer to jackhammer out
    the cement that dried up because he forgot
        to keep the barrel rotating
    or lose his job.
Tell it to the Bushmen who refuse to become farmers
    saying—"Why should we plant when there are
        so many mongo mongo nuts in the world?"

What Every Boy Knows

Every boy knows what it's like
      when he's really alone,
When it's safe to jack off with a passion,
When it's safe to take off his clothes
      and prance around
And parade his lubricating cock
      before every mirror in the house,
Safe to cry out and talk dirty
      while jerking it,
Really scream "I'm coming!"
      when he comes,
Really stand on his head
      and jack off in his face
      if he wants,
Yes, every boy knows
      when it's safe.

At the country picnic the 12-year-old boy
      wanders off by himself in the woods,
      he knows the perfect spot.
On his study-hall break to the library
      the 13-year-old stops in the empty john,
      just enough time for a quickie.
The 14-year-old boyscout waits till he's sure
      everyone in the tent is sleeping,
      quietly, slowly he plays with his dream.
The 15-year-old runs home from school,
      half-way he's already hard,
His heart is pounding
      when he opens the front door,
He knows he's got a full hour
      before his sister or parents return,
Enough time to give himself
      a real workout in the bathtub.
The 16-year-old wakes up in the snowy night,
      with a flashlight he watches himself
      magically masturbate under the comforter.
The 17-year-old puts *Leaves of Grass* aside,
      leans back on the chair with his feet on the wall
      in the basement at home where he studies,
He likes poetry, but right now
      he needs a good handjob
      before he can continue...
No one can see me now, the boy chuckles to himself

And I'm not fool enough anymore to think God
        is watching me horrified
        and will sentence me to hell.
If God doesn't love to watch boys jack off
        as much as boys love to watch themselves jack off
        he does not exist.
The 18-year-old boy licks his lips
        as he jacks off in the hayloft,
If anyone saw me they'd think I was nuts
        he thinks as he squirms and groans.
His devilish lasciviousness to make love to himself
        makes the monkeys at the zoo seem prudes,
There's no posture, no expression on his face,
        no possible method of touch he won't try
        to make it feel more Wow.
The voluptuous 19-year-old knows
        he's got the whole beach to himself today,
He basks naked in the sun,
        then floating on the lake
        gives himself the best handjob of his life.
The 20-year-old mountainclimber still digs the thrill
        of doing it on top of a mountain alone,
He never tells anyone about it, it's a secret
        he keeps to himself,
He still smiles remembering the first time
        he jacked off from a cliff,
Ecstatic boyhood semen spurting and spurting
        thousands of feet
        into the wild valley below....

Lucky Trees

Each year a tree gets new genitals,
And not just one, but thousands:
Some trees have hundreds of thousands
      of penises,
Some trees have hundreds of thousands
      of vaginas,
Some have hundreds of thousands
      of penises and vaginas—
Whereas a human being only gets one—
One vagina or one penis
That's born and grows to puberty,
      blossoms, exults in ripeness,
      slowly withers and dies.

To think a Redwood that's 2000 years old
Gets hundreds of thousands of fresh new
Perfectly formed young male and female
      genital flowers every year
      that mate to become cones,
Cones with seeds in them as virile
      as when at age 70
The Redwood was first able
      to bear mature seeds—
Whereas by the time we're 70
Our seeds' virility, quantity, trajectory
      is past
And each year decrescendos toward death
The beauty, potency, majesty
      of our genital blooms.

But then a tree's seeds are not really seeds—
The seeds that fall from a tree
      are not really seeds,
But embryos! The seeds were
      pollen on anthers on stamens
         of tree flowers
That wind, insect or bird
      jostled or carried
         to the female flower's
      stigma on a style
Where semen joined ovum to form
      embryo which grew
Till ready to be implanted
      in motherearthwomb—

For the earth is every tree's mother,
For the earth is an infinite vagina
        out of which every tree comes.

Yet as we go through our mother's vagina
        when we're born,
Tree's embryos that are eaten
Go through a bird or animal's
        digestive system to be born,
So a tree's vagina a tree baby emerges from
That delivers the tree baby is
A mouth-esophagus-stomach-intestine-anus-tube
        out of which it is shit into earth
Out of which (the final and ultimate
        mothervagina)
It finally bursts into being.

Lucky trees, so different from us,
Would that we were so lucky,
Would that we grew new boyhood cocks
        and girlhood cunts
No matter how old we were every spring.
Would that we could grow to be
        2000 years old
And still make love with our
        hundreds of thousands of
                penises and vaginas—
Ah, that we had as our birthcanal
        the digestive system of a doe
And the moist rich black warm earth
        where she shit her beautiful turds.

Everything Is Different Now

Everything is different now,
Now that I know that octopus penises detach
      and wander alone through the Ocean
           seeking a mate,
So that right now, and throughout
      all human history,
           and millions of years before
      humans were even at
           the tree-shrew level,
Octopus penises wandered alone
      without eyes or ears or noses
           through vast vastnesses
              of Ocean
           searching for a lady-love.

River Anatomy

The mouth of the river
    is really the anus of the river
For the river starts on the mountaintop
      so the mountaintop is the mouth of the river,
        or the cloud is the mouth of the river.
Where the river empties into the sea
    is the anus of the river
      not the mouth of the river,
Unless the river is vomiting into the sea.
But the anus of the river
    is really the penis of the river,
      because what empties into the sea
    is liquid not solid.
So the mouth of the river
    is the penis of the river,
      the vulva of the river.

Privy To My Thoughts

The shit of mice and voles
  contains fungus from truffles they ate
    which contains microorganisms
        without which
      the colossal Douglas Firs
  wouldn't be able to take in and keep
    more water in their root-hairs
      in the dry seasons
    without which they'd die.
No Avenue of Giants without mice-shit!
No stupendous towering treetrunk longevities
  without turds,
    little turds of shy
  scurrying pink-toed and white-whiskered
    pink-nosed mousies.
Ah, wee and cowering timorous beastie,
  what awe-inspiring power
    is in thy feces!

Proving What?

How in autumn, even before the leaves fall,
When they're all at their height of color,
Next year's leaves are already there, tiny,
        on either side of the stem of each leaf
            where it meets its branch,
Already there, waiting,
Before the leaf that is still there
        is dead and falls,
Tiny folded leafbudsheath
Resembling two hands in prayer
Palm to palm with fingers extended.

Proving what?
Life after death exists
        even before you're dead.

Or how when a Redwood tree is cut down or blown over
It doesn't die: because the roots
Curl up out of the earth and become
        new trees,
Each of which can grow to be
Just as tall just as old
        as the tree which was there before.
It'd be as if you were cut off at the ankles
And your top taken away to make hot-tubs,
And your toes curled into the ground and came up
        as ten new "you"s—looking exactly like you
            and being exactly you.
And so a Redwood you see now that's 2000 years old
        may've come from the root of a Redwood that was
                2000 years old
        that may've come from the root of a Redwood that was
                2000 years old
        so far back it's literally one million years old!
And that's why they're called *Sequoia sempervirens*,
        ever-living.

Proving...what?
Even before you're dead
        life after death exists.

Happenstance

She paraded naked before him
      to tantalize and tease him.
Plant roots follow paths blazed by worms.
Worms eat their way through the soil.
Children sleep like rivers in their beds,
      dreamflowing.
Two snowflakes touch as they fall.
Creekgurgle and lakelapping
      in an old man's ears.
Old woman senile in nursinghome
      humming jingles from
      long-ago TV commercials.
A single granule of jackpine pollen
      floating at 2000 feet
      among tumultuous cumulus.
Debussy daydreaming the girl
      with the flaxen pubic hair.
Porcupine alone in treetop
      swaying in the wind
      nibbling young maple-leaf shoots.
Backpacker discovers fawnskull
      beside Memengwa Creek.
Countless dead leaves
      pierced by countless
      green grass blades.
A 10-million-year-old fossil raindrop impression
      in a museum.
Listening to a conch shell in a spaceship
      on your way to the moon.

Boyhood Waterfall Offering

Communioning with waterfall splendor
    in the spurt of growth called youth,
Sprawling naked on overhanging cedar
    drenched in billowing mist
Jacking off into rainbow'd spray,
Spurting burgeoning boyseeds
    into plummeting gush,
Blending puberty orgasmcry
    with thundering plunge,
Actually seeing your semen
    disappear into huge
    deluging white,
Contributing an ejaculation
    from the waterfall of boycome
    given your boyhood form
Into a Waterfall Reality
    that's been ejaculating
Before America was America,
Before Russia was Russia,
Before China was China,
Before Stonehenge and Pyramids—
    better than jacking off in a Bible,
    better than jerking off in a Dictionary,
    better than jagging off in pornomag papertowel,
    better than confessional or communion wafer,
No eternal spirit without eternal spurt!!!!!!!!!!
Shouldn't every boy jack off into a waterfall
    before he becomes a man?
Shouldn't every wilderness have secret falls
    visionary youths can hike to to make love to
    sighing seeing their white drops flying
    into waterfall-splurge?
Shouldn't youths bring their cocks and balls
    to waterfall-brink
    to splurt their semen as a gift
    like Wise Men bringing gifts to the Christ-child?
(Aren't waterfalls magnets pulling sexy boys
    to smoke solitude marijuana
    by their wilderness aura
    and jerk off into tumult colossal?)
Why?
Because you get high being around a being
    that's been spurting continually for millennia,
A being whose roaring comecry
    has not stopped once in 10,000 years.

Hot Summer Night Rendezvous

The two boys embracing in the thunderstorm
Don't care if they get drenched,
Don't care if as they strip each other
    their clothes drop in lightninglight
        into puddles
    and are kicked laughingly into the mud.
It's the first time they've kissed each other,
The first time either of them ever kissed
    a boy
And neither has ever kissed
    a girl
And neither ever kissed before
    with his tongue.
They had no idea
    how passionate
        passion could be—
    they can hardly believe it,
That merely putting their lips together
    could be so...
        ah.
For a moment they stand apart
    silently gazing at each other
        in the flashes and thunder,
Centuries of Boyhood, Aeons of BoyLove
    proud in their playful smiles,
Knowing just what they're going to do,
    even though they never did it before,
Knowing that before long
    each of them is going to jack off
        the first boy he ever jacked off
    besides himself,
Knowing both of them can come
    and, giving in, give themselves
        to boyfriendship's topsecret gesture,
Knowing they both know
    how to jack off real good
        and aren't going to stop frenching
    while they whimper toward the brink.
Sure, it's beautiful
    to see a boy you love
        ejaculate in the lightning in the rain,
Crying with pleasure while the thunder thunders
    and the sky ejaculates millions of raindrops
As you squirm in rapture
    on the muddy grass
        under the tossing trees.

Blowjobscope

When we look into space
    we look back in time,
When we give a blowjob
    we suck eternity.
Erections are telescopes!
Look through with your mouth
    instead of your eyes!
Your mouth can suck better
    than your eyes can see!
Your nose can smell more
    while blowing a boy
    than your eyes see gaping galaxies!
Give blowjobs to exploding universe!
Give blowjobs to boypenises whose atoms were created
    billions of years ago in stars that lived and died
    before the Sun and Earth existed!
Every spermcell is a star.
Every ejaculation is a galaxy.
Cocksuckers are astronomers
    as much as astronomers!
Look through the most powerful telescope on Earth
    and see the stars come in your eyes
    but put your lips to the eyepiece
    nothing happens.
Who gives a blowjob tastes the stars,
Tastes the birth of stars, planets, life,
    joy, sorrow, death, eternity!
Suddenly a world of pure energy
    flashes into being!
Give blowjobs to the faint afterglow
    of the origin of the Universe!
Sucking a boy off with pure love
    is cosmic gazing starry nightsky.

Tell the Judge

Tell the judge you were ravished by a rainbow!
Tell the judge the sunrise took advantage of you!
Tell the judge the starrynightsky
    seduced you and raped you repeatedly
        in every orifice!
Tell the judge the Sequoias buttfucked you
    before Christ was born
        and are still buttfucking you!
Tell the judge the Wilderness showed you
    pornographic panoramas
        and tried to get you to come
    to its house to get you high
        and suck you off while you looked at them
    all afternoon!
Tell the judge the wild rose drugged you with its smell
    so you couldn't help what you did!
Tell the judge the waterfall forced you to suck its cock
    and swallow its come!
Tell the judge the soaring eagle exposed itself to you
    and you've never been the same since!
Tell the judge the view from the mountaintop
    forced you to jack off in its face!

Your Honor

Your honor the orchid deflowered me.
Your honor the tree-shade fondled me indecently.
Your honor the summer morning forest smell
     after a rainy night
        assaulted and molested me.
Your honor the caressing wind gave me a boner.
Your honor the sun abused me through my wet swimsuit
     as I lay sunbathing
        so when I got up everyone stared.
Your honor the moonlight jacked me off
     when I went camping.
Your honor the moonlight moonlight I swear it moonlight
     spurted from my moonlit dick.
Your honor I swear on this Blowjob Bible
     the clouds exposed
        their buttocks and breasts to me
     more than Yahweh exposed his buttocks to Moses.
Your honor the spectacular sunset beat me up
     on my way home from work
        and stole my work ethic and identity cards.
Your honor the night stole the daylight
     from my house.
Your honor my loved ones are keeping me prisoner
     in a coffin underground just 'cause I'm dead.
Your honor these maggots are eating my dead body
     without my permission.
Your honor don't corpses have any rights?

Underwater Lake Michigan Socrates

Thought of dropping bust of Socrates
        Morgan Gibson gave me
                that belonged to his dead
        Congregationalist minister father
Over the side of the *Spartan* carferry
        into the middle of Lake Michigan
                as it crosses
        from Ludington to Milwaukee,
No shore visible in any direction, no one on deck,
        so cold—even in July—but I thought
                in advance to bring wool cap,
        wool shirt, gloves, scarf
                and downfilled jacket—
Lightblue clear sky, windy,
        darkblue waters spreading white-capt
                and screaming wheeling gulls,
        the ship rolling in wavetroughs stolidly—
Possibility the bust might plummet downward head up,
        land perfectly balanced on
                underwater cliff edge
        so it overlooks vast underwater valley
                and deepwater fish
        come to inspect it
                while all my life goes on
        and the history of humankind goes on.
How many busts of Socrates exist
        contemplating the bottom of Lake Michigan?

Waterfallsexual

Actually I'm a waterfallsexual—
Ejaculating cocks only
            one kind of waterfall I love.
Leaves coming forth in spring another.
Leaves falling in fall another.
Snow, rain, moonlight, dusk, dawn another.
Wildflowers bursting up blooming another.
Vegetables and fruit ejaculating from the earth
            into my mouth and out my asshole
            into the earth another.
What can you expect from a poet
            Nature exposed herself to?
What greater exhibitionist is there?

Pussysmell Candlelight

Lighting the candle that was in your cunt,
The pink candle I twirled carefully exquisitely
       in and out your velvet vagina,
The candle I smelled later
       your inner pussyaroma aura,
The candle, one of five I made in sixth grade,
       dipping my wick in and out
          deep vats of melted wax,
       giving them to my mother for Christmas
          she saving them rediscovering them
       thirty years later giving them back to me
Me alone in my tent in the wilderness
       night howling storm
          rain plummeting dark November
       burning them, candles made
          before I even knew or guessed
       wilderness existed,
Before a single orgasm blessed me,
Before I knew how babies were made
       or discovered my tinkler
          my little weiner
       could grow huge and I
          could spurt myself for joy
       in the mirror,
Before I ever dreamed I'd love boys
       and live with my boyfriend 22 years before
          age 41
       experience my first naked girlfriend ecstasy,
And the last candle remaining sensuously played with
       in and out my first girlfriend
          of my life's vagina,
Now yellow flame illuminating
       my darkened writingroom
Me here alone writing
       by pussycandlesmell light
Smoking a joint dedicated
       to the wilderness
And all the times we made love.

Pussy Feels Like

Her pussy feels like a tofu hotdog
    on a 100% whole wheat bun.
Her pussy feels like a box of crayons
    melting in the sun.
Her pussy feels like being in a balloon
    before the invention of the airplane
        smoking hashish looking down.
Her pussy feels like distant wind-chimes.
Her pussy feels velvety as a sumac bud,
    soft as a trillium petal,
        soft as the white underside
    of a darkgreen poplar leaf.
Her pussy feels like cooing mourning doves,
    sparkle on sunny water, rainbow spray
        above a misty waterfall, playful surf
    and warm pure sand, rippling fields of grain,
        flickering leafshade, cloudshadows
    moving quickly over canyonlands at dawn.
Her pussy feels like shafts of light
    in redwood dusk, barefoot feet
        in sucking muck
    rustle of golden aspen leaves
    in lazy blue September.
Her pussy feels like the little whirlpools
    left by the rower's pulled oars.
Her pussy feels like a thoroughbred filly
    running free for miles over moonlit prairie,
        eyes wild, nostrils flaring,
    floating mane and tail.
Her pussy feels like swimming in the lake as a boy
    your mother on shore yelling come out now
        you begging five minutes more
    she letting you dive
        a dozen more times off the pier
    splashing laughing leaping
        up the ladder grinning.
Her pussy feels like being rocked by your mother as a child
    in a rockingchair at night in a thunderstorm
        while lullabied softly to sleep
    told everything will be okay
        as lightning lightnings, thunder thunders
    downpour comes pouring down.
Her pussy feels like being tucked in by your mother
    on Christmas Eve in a blizzard believing

Santa will come down the chimney
with all the gifts you ever dreamed.
Her sleek and silky sulky sassy pussy
feels like the pussy of a teenage girl
that wants and needs to be fucked.

Dachau Stone

Stone from Dachau come to my writingroom
    as gift for me
From woman visiting me who visited Dachau
    and returned with this stone
        she found there,
    just happened to bend over
    and pick up,
Thought I'd find it interesting
    considering deathcamp references
        in my poetry,
"Thought Antler might write a poem
    about it."
On holding a stone from Dachau in Milwaukee,
    I wonder how many poets this instant
        are holding a stone
    from Dachau
        in Milwaukee or the World?
Could be I'm the only one.
Could be I'm the only person on Earth this instant
    contemplating in their hand
        a Dachau stone.
Boot-shaped stone, purple in color,
    on whose sole a ghostly white splotch
        shaped like wraith-like
    winding-sheet
        attached to skull face
    screaming voiceless horrorgape.
Stone from Dachau thousands gassed there walked on,
    their anguished corpses ovened or dumped
        in open mass graves
    making liberators vomit
        and weep uncontrollably.
Stone from Dachau come to Milwaukee chamber
    of Antler in Eternity, into the room
        where he lives and breathes,
    into the secret laboratory
        of visionary sexpoems
    and marijuana hymns written for the utopias
        of 21st Century and beyond.
Stone from that point on Earth of inhumanity's epitome
    come to be shrined beside
        ceremonial wilderness stones
    brought back as talismans
To console citybound me getting stoned

and placing them on my heart
or forehead
remembering the wilds
where they found me—
That wild freedom and joy
compared to the suffering and cruelty
memento'd by this stone.

Anthem

Not standing when "Star-Spangled Banner" played
      by Milwaukee Symphony in outdoor amphitheater
            beside Lake Michigan near downtown Milwaukee
      before the Beethoven's Ninth concert,
Everyone else standing, everyone else singing,
Putting my head in one hand as it plays so heroic,
Thinking of all the Persian Gulf War dead,
      Iraqi soldiers buried alive in trenches
            or strafed as they retreated,
      women and children bombed in Baghdad airraidshelter,
            the 20-year-old from Wauwatosa
      killed by "friendly fire" on my birthday,
Thinking of My Lai, Wounded Knee, Dresden, Nagasaki,
Thinking back to Washington Park bandshell
      20 years ago Vietnam War era
One summer eve "The Star-Spangled Banner"
      played before *Pagliacci*
And not standing then, everyone standing,
      not singing then, everyone singing,
Remembering the hateful threats and curses whispered
      behind me.
Now no curses or threats, only singing sadly and sweetly
      mothers and fathers whose voices seem
            soft-spoken and sorrowful too
      as if they think me Vietnam Veteran
            remembering his bestfriend killed there
      and remember their bestfriend
            killed in World War II or Korea,
No tone of defiant patriotism to my ears,
No growl of rage in the melody
Only a sound of many melancholy voices trying
      to sound cheerful, hopeful, trying
            to believe we still are
      the great nation we were taught we were
            and thought we were
      in gradeschool,
No tone of hate or scorn—as if they understand
      why I will never stand
            for "The Star-Spangled Banner"
      or the American Flag again.
America became Ecotopia and Ecotopia's flag is the Wilderness
      and Ecotopia's National Anthem is the wind.
America loved itself so much
      it became Ecotopia

                    after all.
Now we play no National Anthem
And need no Symphony or amphitheater
            or downtown or Milwaukee
As we sit and listen to crickets
            and watch fireflies as it gets dark
                    in hot July along the pure fresh-water shores
            of Great Lake Michigan.

Draft-Dodgers vs. Poetry-Dodgers

Rather than fulfilling their military obligation,
    fulfilling their poetry obligation—
After all, what's more fulfilling,
    learning how to kill or love?
Those who become soldiers
    are evading the Poetry Service—
    dodging the Poetry Draft.
Isn't it their duty to their Country
    more to become a poet
    than a brainwashed murder robot?
When the young contemplate what branch of the Service
    to join,
They should know they can contemplate
    joining Poetry,
That Poetry is a Service that serves
    the realization of Utopia
    more than becoming skilled
    at killing.
Too long it was thought the young were needed
    to go to war,
Now the young are needed to go to peace.
Now the young are needed to go to poetry.

American History In Context

500,000 years ago sleepy chipmunks
    snuggled in their burrows.
400,000 years ago doe
    nibbled ladyslipper.
300,000 years ago
    dust on tiger swallowtail wing.
200,000 years ago
    whirligig beetle whirligigged.
100,000 years ago
    blue heron still as a statue.
50,000 years ago
    male seahorse belly-pouch
        swollen with herd of
    perfectly shaped baby seahorses.
25,000 years ago
    leopard frog on lilypad.
10,000 years ago
    male wasp stroking female wasp antennae
        lightly with his mouthparts
    as they copulate on the wing
        from flower to flower.
Right now hippo shitting and pissing
    while whirling its tail like a propeller
        scattering the mess in all directions.
10,000 years from now
    opossum scurries across
        overgrown road.
25,000 years from now
    lobsters grappling lobsters
        with giant chelae.
50,000 years from now
    alligator snapper huge mouth agape
        wriggling pink worm-like tongue
    to attract unwary fish.
100,000 years from now
    female praying mantis clasps her mate
        eating his eyes and head
    causing headless corpse to writhe and kick
        till it inserts penis and pumps
    as she continues eating him
        till nothing's left
    but his penis still ejaculating
        in her ovipositor.
200,000 years from now

yellow pollen-laden anthers
    of a red columbine.
300,000 years from now
    a white pine in spring
        smells just as good.
400,000 years from now
    a black bear sighs
        in her hibernation den.
500,000 years from now sleepy chipmunks
    snuggle in their burrows.

Ultimatum

Unless England, France, Spain, Portugal, Holland
    un-invade North and South America
        by 1650 A.D.,
    India's deadline,
India will attack and force them to go back
    so the Passage to India won't have to be
        a Trail of Tears to Wounded Knee.

Unless pioneers westering from Alleghenies
    stop extincting Buffalo
        and return to the East Coast
    by Crazy Horse's deadline,
The Sioux will attack prairie schooner factories
    and coalmines being dug to provide
        steam for transcontinental railroad.

Unless gringos withdraw
    from Texas and California
        by Mexico and Spain's deadline,
Mexico and Spain will attack Texas and California
    and storm Guantanamo base yelling
    "Remember the *Maine*
        and Santa Anna's wooden leg!"

Unless U.S. withdraw T.R.'s big stick
    from Central America's rear-end
        by Brazil and Argentina's deadline,
    Brazil and Argentina
Will blitzkrieg U.S. with their secret weapon
    of cloned Nazi refugees
        more fun than a barrel of Hitlers.

Unless Brazil stops butchering rainforest
    a footballfield per second
        by Thoreau's deadline,
John Brown's ghost
    will go to the Amazon
        and lead the Yanomami
    to blowgun poisondarts at chainsaw massacre-ers.

Unless China bring back to life the 2000
    democracy-demanding students
        and their Statue of Liberty
By the Dalai Lama's deadline,

Nepal will bomb them nonstop
with hashish templeballs.

Unless U.S. stop acid-rain murder
of Canada lake-forest wilderness
by Canada's deadline,
The Mounties will charge
Pittsburgh and Detroit
toppling smokestacks
and pouring maplesyrup in gastanks.

Unless cigarets withdraw their cancer from
lungs of ten million who die yearly
smoking them,
Black Elk will return to turn cigarets into calumets
and turn tobacco fields
into fields of hemp
to treat the glaucoma and carcinoma
of a Growth Economy.

Sweet-Talk

Sweet-talk Christianity out of fellatiophobia.
Sweet-talk Capitalism out of work-ethic.
Sweet-talk Communism out of thought-police.
Sweet-talk cigarets into marijuana.
Sweet-talk hamburgers into tofu
     and sugar into honey.
Sweet-talk gasoline into tamari.
Sweet-talk shoppingcenters from gobbling up farmland,
     parkinglots from gobbling up parkland,
          skyscrapers from gobbling up sky.
Sweet-talk populationbomb from imploding
     our vast territorial space.
Sweet-talk condominiums to turn into wigwams,
     nuclearbombs to turn into birchbark canoes.
Sweet-talk torture devices to become food for starving children.
Sweet-talk double-agents to become infinite-agents.
Sweet-talk star-wars weaponry into 100% maple syrup.
Sweet-talk sweethearts in sweatshops to sweet-talk
     billionaires to share their fortune with us.
Sweet-talk sweet-stalks of sweet-flag to talk us
     into lifelong friendship.
Sweet-talk pornomags to transform into living flesh.
Butter-up every kernel on the cob of sweet-corn.
Sweet-talk bullets that killed back into their guns.
Sweet-talk bombs that fell back into their planes
     back into their factories back into their metals
         in the Earth.
Sweet-talk bombardments into bardbombardments.
Sweet-talk avalanches and floods to reverse.
Sweet-talk hurricanes and earthquakes to calm down.
Sweet-talk downpour to the drought.
Sweet-talk sight to the blind, hearing to the deaf,
     skin to the burned, health to the ill,
         healing to the wound, knit to the bone.
Sweet-talk the machete out of Dian Fossey's brain.
Sweet-talk Hart Crane from the propeller.
Sweet-talk life to the dead.
Sweet-talk Immortality to the dead.
Sweet-talk Death's prophetic ear to secret rivuletgurgle spot
     in virgin climax hemlock towering quietude.
Sweet-talk street-talk, beat-talk and tea-talk
     to willow-murmur, pine-sough, aspen-quiver,
         maple-rustle, oak-moan, elder-sigh.
Sweet-talk *International Businessman's Who's Who*

to the sages of the ages in their pages.
Sweet-talk cocaine kingpins into springdawn earthsmell.
Sweet-talk microchip zealots fathom Anasazi relics.
Sweet-talk terrorism into tourism, tourism into pantheism,
          pantheism into panting jism.
Sweet-talk factorypoisons out of our water, air, earth, blood,
          mother's milk and father's sperm.
Sweet-talk clearcuts and crewcuts
          into old-growth and long hair.
Sweet-talk oil-spills to slurp back in.
Sweet-talk endangered species from extinction.
Sweet-talk extinct species to return.
Sweet-talk purports of rapport to tumuli of avatars.
Sweet-talk skyrocketing economic price index
          into star-gazing, star-blazing, star-amazing.
Boomerang all Voodoos! Boomerang all Voodoos!
Sweet-talk the trembling human being on the suicide window-ledge
          to come back inside
                    though the huge crowd below
          screams—"Jump."

Kicking the Habit

Factories enter drug treatment programs
     to be cured of their chemical dependence.
Nuclear plants enter drug treatment programs
     to be cured of their substance abuse.
Cars enter drug treatment programs
     to be cured of being gasoline junkies.
Nicotine junkies enter drug treatment programs
     to be talked out of suicide cancer.
Miners enter drug treatment programs
     to be cured of being stripmine addicts.
Loggers enter hug-tree programs
     to be cured of being clearcut addicts.
Slaughterhouses enter drug treatment programs
     to be cold-turkey'd of their slaughter addiction.
Wall Street enters drug treatment programs
     to be detoxed from stockmarket habit.
Megalopolises enter drug treatment programs
     to kick their skyscraper habit.
Monopolists enter white-collar thug treatment programs
     to be cured of being hooked on profit.
Drug czars enter herbal-treat programs
     to be cured of marijuanaphobia.
Fundamentalists enter de-bigotry programs
     to be cured of homophobia.
Supertankers enter drug treatment programs
     to be cured of their oil-spill habit.
Smokestacks enter drug treatment programs
     to be cured of their acid-rain habit.
Toxic wastes enter drug treatment programs
     to be cured of groundwater pollution habit.
Guns enter drug treatment programs
     to be exorcised of their homicide habit.
Boys and men undergo fellatio therapy
     to cure them of overpopulation habit.
Women and girls undergo cunnilingus therapy
     to cure them of overpregnancy habit.
Arms merchants enter drug treatment programs
     to be cured of their mass-murder habit.

Factory Sacrifice

Factories volunteer to be thrown into the volcano
    so the acid-rain typhoon won't come.
Factories leap on the live grenade of industrialism
    to save their buddies, us.
Factories wander away in a blizzard
    because they've become a burden
        on the tribe.
Factories give themselves to be crucified
    so all who believe in them
        can relax forever.
Factories immolate themselves
    on the work-ethic's funeral pyre.
Factories have to be cut off below the knee
    to save the leg.
Factories serenely cease to be
    after drinking cups of hemlock
        surrounded by philosophers.
Factories help workers get into lifeboats
    and then nobly go down with the ship.
Factories find work so meaningless
    they dream of being torn down
        even before they're built.
Factories pull out their life-support system
    on their own
        and are discovered dead
    by the nurse.
Garlanded by flowers, factories ascend
    the pyramid at dawn
        to have their machines torn out
    held up dripping grease
        to the Sun.

Job Replacement For Loggers
of Old Growth

1. Be paid the same amount to do Tai Chi eight hours a day
    on the giant stumps.
2. Be paid twice as much to smoke marijuana eight hours a day
    sitting under thousand-year-old trees
        meditating their longevity, beauty, reality.
3. Be paid three times as much to become a medium
    conducting séances for cut-down trees
        to see what their thoughts are now.
4. Be paid four times as much to plant trees—
    to re-Sequoia America, to re-White Pine, re-Chestnut, re-Elm,
        re-Oak, re-Maple, re-Birch, re-Redwood America.
5. Be paid five times as much to tree-spike every tree
    in the Pacific Northwest.
6. Be paid six times as much to Ghost Dance oldgrowth old ways
    back to our clearcut souls.
7. Be paid seven times as much to hold mice by the tails
    so northern spotted owls swoop
        and snatch them
    upward on silent wings
        to hungry owlets in the nest.
8. Get paid eight times as much to hike forest mountain trails
    25 miles a day.
9. Get paid nine times as much to turn sawmills
    into schools, libraries, hospitals,
        artist studios, homeless shelters.
10. Get paid ten times as much to turn chainsaws
    into rainbows, bulldozers into dozing wolves,
        logging trucks into grizzlies.
11. Get paid eleven times as much to learn wilderness birdsongs
    and sing them on busy streetcorners
        to passersby.
12. Get paid twelve times as much to learn
    how to make love 8 hours a day
        and for boys and men to learn
    how to have 30 orgasms an hour like the male rhino
        who ejaculates an amount of sperm
    the size of a human body
        without once losing his erection.
13. Get paid thirteen times as much to learn to communicate
    with mosquitos and blackflies and teach them
        not to bite us anymore.
14. Get paid fourteen times as much to photograph snowflakes
    and enlarge the photos and create

        book after book of
   enlarged snowflake designs.
15. Be paid fifteen times as much to make earrings
     of fossilized dinosaur bone marrow in which
         individual fossilized red blood cells
     are visible.
16. Be paid sixteen times as much to remove roads from Eden,
     starting with Yosemite and Yellowstone.
17. Be paid seventeen times as much to become
     muralist, harpist, pianist and play
        Chopin to chipmunks—
     preludes in spring, etudes in summer,
        nocturnes in fall, waltzes in winter.
18. Be paid eighteen times as much to create skyscraper-sized
     replicas of Michelangelo's David in the Sahara.
19. Be paid nineteen times as much to repeat over and over
     to the statue of the passenger pigeon:
        "Red eye of loon, orange eye of oriole,
     yellow eye of eagle, green eye of hummingbird,
        blue eye of cormorant, purple eye of owl,
     brown eye of duck, black eye of chickadee,
        white eye of towhee, gold eye of bittern."
20. Be paid twenty times as much to write poetry
     that monkeywrenches ecocidal mindsets
        and decommissions forever
     fundamentalist Christianity.
21. Be paid twenty-one times as much to learn
     how to give good foot massage and
        make good oatmeal cookies and
     how to play the harmonica
        in a wistful way.

Poetry Boom In Milwaukee

There's a Poetry Boom in Milwaukee!
More people joining the Poetry Force because
    unlimited employment opportunities abound!
The estimated number of poets here
    was 86 in 1986,
Well above a low of 3 in 1846.
If the present rate of increase continues,
    2000 Milwaukee poets by the year 2000!
Upheavals in new poem possibilities
    have created a need for
    myriads of bards.
Experts predict high demand for poets
    could lead to a poet power shortage,
    especially for erotic poem poets.
Soon politicians will be wooing
    endorsement from the Poets' Union
    more than AFL-CIO.
At this rate it won't be long before
    rather than the State of Wisconsin
    gives General Motors
    9 million in taxpayer money
    to open a new truck plant
    and create 900 new jobs,
The State gives 9 million
    so 900 more poets can be free
    to work on 900 new books of poems.

Dream

Applied for and got grants from Wisconsin Arts Board,
    NEA, Guggenheim
To learn how to counterfeit money
    and hand it out to poor people everywhere
And so much publicity surrounded me
The MacArthur Foundation awarded me a hundred million a year
    to open up centers for unemployed workers
        in every city
    to learn how to counterfeit money
        not only for themselves
    but for the sick, starving, deranged, addicted, suicidal
        everywhere
And so much publicity surrounded me
I ran for President on the platform
    everyone would get a free counterfeiting machine
        and be encouraged to counterfeit money
    not only for themselves
        but for everyone
    and got elected
And so much publicity surrounded me
People believed I was the Savior
    till some infidel who believed
        poor oppressed people a necessity
    assassinated me
And so much publicity surrounded it
    my face was voted to be
        the only face on money
    and the religion of everyone being rich and happy
        took over the world
And so much publicity surrounded it
    God, who'd been sleeping since creating life,
        was awakened by all the happy laughter
    and moans of ecstasy
        and was so delighted to see and hear
    such naked joy
He/She thought to itself
    maybe Immortality isn't such a bad idea after all
        and decided to let everyone on Earth
    live forever.

Milking the Raspberry Cow

Each July morning I'm to be found
    in my backyard milking
        my raspberry bush.
Just like a cow
    it waits to be milked
        till greeny udder
    spurts red berries,
        fun, fun.
Able to see now how
Paleolithic people could live by
    hunting and gathering.
"The women would pick berries"—
    ha, I used to think, ha,
        pick berries?
    as if you could live on berries!
Apologies to you berry-pickers of yore!
Forgive me for not knowing
Just how much comes
    from a single bush!
In one month my raspberry cow produced
    $167 worth of berries!
(I gloat to know the market price per half-pint.)
I feel proud like a bird in an Audubon print
    with lush berry branches surrounding me,
Early, still aura'd by my dreams,
    each pick a decision on ripeness
        and rightness—
    no wormy berries or unripe,
        no squishy over-ripe acceptable.
The feel of just enough pull to pluck them,
    so little, yet actual, gentle,
Coming loose in your hand, fragrant, sunwarmed,
    actually warm from the heat of the light
        of the big close star
    that caused them to swell
        to gem-like perfection,
Proving to me
    how good to be buried
        and come back as berries!
I've eaten more raspberries in four weeks
    than in the last forty years!
Every one of which I gathered myself
    in ancient berry-gathering ritual,
Gobbling so many thankful mouthfuls I'm almost

ashamed of myself, but not really—
an amount devoured greater
than the volume of my body!
A raspberry man milking a raspberry cow,
I've never been raspberries more than now!

Oh-Oh

Birds decide to give up their wings
      because flying indulges in an ego trip.
Hermit crabs decide they have to pay rent
      on their shells.
Snakes invent banks where they can invest
      their sloughed-off skins.
Beavers vote to build highrise lodges
      above their ponds.
Squirrels expect a minimum wage
      for storing nuts in secret.
Earthworm expressways install periodic tollbooths
      to help defray construction costs.
Lions build cages, lock themselves in
      and charge admission to see them.
Butterflies get rich from fee to see
      emergence from chrysalis.
Termite Thoreau goes to live by a dewdrop for awhile
      before returning to the termite mound.
The turnip and parsnip form a partnership.
Celery wants a salary.
Cows demand humans make their own milk
      from their own tits
      and eat their own sawn muscles.
Trees agree to sprout money instead of leaves
      as long as they can make newspapers out of human corpses
      to print tree news.
Dust motes go on strike
      for safer floating conditions.
One raindrop says to another raindrop—
      "I don't believe in clouds
      or that we're falling."
Plankton plot how to conquer the Ocean.
Seahorses form cavalries and charge
      to periwinkle bugle-calls.
Mayflies scheme to be more famous as poets
      than other mayflies.
Mountains want to get away from it all too,
      tired of carrying the world on their shoulders.
Roses make x-rated videos of rosebuds opening.
Sloths realize they better change their lazy ways
      or else.
Spiders decide not to spin webs
      unless they're displayed in art museums.
Crickets refuse to cricket

unless haikus take notice.
Whales grow back their arms and legs
    so they can return to land and work
    in factories.
Flowers want to work in factories too.
They feel funny just sitting around
    doing nothing but being beautiful
    and smelling good.
Penguins decide to take off their tuxedos
    and wear their bum-clothes for a change.

Somewhere Along the Line

What interested me most about gorillas
    when I first studied them
Was not that the males' penises are only
    two inches long,
But that gorillas shit and piss in their beds
    and don't leave to relieve themselves
        (though they build new beds every day),
Also they eat their feces—yes,
    they eat their turds.
And this made me realize that we
    (somewhere along the line)
Decided we wouldn't shit and piss in our beds,
We agreed we wouldn't eat our shit
    or drink our piss,
That we would wear clothes
    and not go naked in public
        and not shit or piss in public
    and not jack off in public,
Not fuck or suck in public,
Not stick our fingers up our rear-ends
    and smell them
        (even in the privacy
    of our own homes),
Or on meeting another of our kind
    sniff each other's cock and balls
        and cunt and asshole like a dog
    but shake hands like a man
And rather than pissing and shitting to mark
    our territory
We invented money
And rather than gathering food from plants
    we'd work to plant them raise them sell them
And rather than killing animals fish birds
    with our mouths and eating them
        raw and bloody
We'd hire others of our kind
    to kill them
        and cut them up in little pieces
    not with their mouths
        but with sharp knives in their hands,
And somewhere we decided rather than live in trees
    we'd kill them, cut them up in long pieces,
        build houses and live
    inside them while sitting in chairs

made from them and write poems
about them on paper made from them
　　with a pencil made from them
about somewhere along the line
　　we decided to be different than
gorillas and monkeys because
　　our way of being was right
because we were better
　　than any other creature on Earth.

Put Your Money Where Your Mouth Is

Put your money where your mouth is.
Put your money where your asshole is.
Put the eyes staring from the pyramidions on dollarbills
       directly over where your eyes are.
Put your money where the blood of the poor
       who sell their blood for money is.
Put your money where the semen of boys
       who sell their semen for money is.
Put your Swiss banks where your Bergen-Belsen is.
Put your profit margin where your
       cannibal consumerism is.
Put your stockmarket where your
       ecocide deathsquads are.
Put your millionaires where your homeless are.
Put your billionaires where your starving millions are.
Put your trillionaires where your mass graves are.
Put your poetry where your mouth is.

Prove To Me

In a single blizzard more snowflakes fall
    than all the money produced
        in the history of the world.
In a single fall more leaves fall
    than all the money produced
        in the history of the world.
In this Universe alone, not counting
    Universes before and after
        and Universes
    concurrent with this Universe,
More planets with Utopias on them exist
    than all the money produced
        in human history.

Explain to me why
    snow can't be used as money.
Explain to me why each fallen leaf
    can't be pecuniary remuneration.
Prove to me beyond the shadow of a doubt
    why the epiphany zillions of planets
        have Utopias on them
    can't be legal tender.

Why can't I fill my cart with food
    and after the girl rings up my bill
        give her a pinecone?
Why can't I knock on my landlord's door
    and hand him a flower
        for rent?
And when the police take me away
    and demand to see my identification
        what else can I do but
    reach into my pocket
And present them
    a handful of sand
        running through my fingers?

From Twilight to Twilight

From standing in late March twilight
    atop Williamson Indian Mound
        rising 150 feet above
    forest meadow creek
        mysterious ancient serene
    near Cedarville, Ohio
        with friends after my reading
    at Wright State
        inhaling thawing earthsmell
    under the stars
        while holding hands
    in silence
        in a circle
    a long time
        before and after
    I whisper—
        "Restore for all"...
To the next evening's twilight
    entering downtown Chicago
        seeing from a Greyhound
    stopped behind
        a long line of cars at a stoplight,
    the world's tallest skyscraper
        purple colossal in the distance,
    while nearby right across from me
        a faded billboard with man
    dressed in business suit
        with the words—
    "When getting ahead in the world
        means the world to you"
    and below, a faded sign
        showing a tombstone
    with the caption—
        "Tombstones made while you wait."

Now You Know

New studies reveal
Male babies get erections in the womb
        on the average of five times a day.
Deeper inside their mother is their little fetus boner
        than their actual father's manly studmeat
                can penetrate,
Closer to their mother's heart
        is their little fetus boner
                than their father's actual giant hard-on
        ever comes.
Too bad, too bad a father can't have
        the miniature living boner of his unborn son
                inside him,
        or the miniature living vagina of his unborn daughter
                inside him.
Too bad a father can't give birth to a penis
        from his penis
                the way a mother can give birth
        to a vagina from her vagina.
If you had time-machine x-ray vision
        you could see inside your mother
                pregnant with you
        the little baby-to-be-that-is-you
                has a boner.
Not till now does it dawn on you
You really had erections before you were born,
That your penis was alive and excitable
        before you even knew what a boy or girl was,
                before you ever saw your face or penis,
        before you ever saw the outside world
                or had a name or personality
        or daydreamed being a bard
                your little member went from limp to hard
        a thousand times
                inside your mother.

Snowflakes

Snowflakes clustered to snowflakes
    falling like skydivers
        holding hands in a circle.
       *

Diamonds buried underground
    like snowflakes suspended
        in dark nightsky.
       *

Turds falling from 6 billion human rumps,
    6 billion snowflakes falling
        from a single cloud.
       *

Incense is snowing
    molecules of scent
        in your meditation room.
       *

Raindrops burst into snowflakes
    like kernals burst
        into popcorn.
       *

Exhibit of folded paper cut-out
    snowflake designs made by children
        200 years ago.
       *

One million ice crystals form a snowflake,
    six million snowflakes form
        a cubic foot of snow.
       *

A cubic foot of snow
    contains as many snowflakes as
        Jews killed in World War II.
       *

Throughout time enough snow has fallen
    to cover the entire globe
        to a depth of 5000 miles.

Thoughts Breathing in a Blizzard

Breathing air with snow falling through it
 thinking how flour is sifted through a sieve
Each different snowflake design is a sieve
 and the air is charged with the energy
  of each snowflake design
   falling through it,
Air passing through the shapes
 of openings in the interior
  of each falling flake
 as well as along the edges,
Serrating in minute invisible architectures
 zillion-shaped clarified vibrancy
  of snowflake sculpture reality
 the edges of snowflake symmetry
  chiselling microscopically
 into an invisible display
  of snowflake-sculptured air
 beyond human comprehension.
And as an animal leaves its track
 in wet sand or mud
  so each snowflake design
 leaves its track
  in cool moist air
 as it falls,
So that in breathing air
 snowflakes have passed through
  you breathe the invisible tracks
 their designs have imprinted
  in the air
And as a hunter follows the bear
 by stepping in its tracks
  you follow the snow
 by breathing the invisible
  patterns of its designs
   pressed into the air
  as it falls.

Snowing Inside Me

Walking through snowstorm, snow
    on hat, shoulders, beard,
I realize it isn't snowing
    inside me.
My body prevents snow
    from falling in it.
It snows around but not in
    my chest, not in
My heart, not in
    my arms or legs.
My eyes see each flake
    and it registers in
My brain
    but the snow is not in
My eyes, not in
    my brain
Is it?

After death, if I die in the woods
    and my body decays where it falls
It could snow in the space
    my lungs took up,
It could snow in the holes
    where my eyes were,
It could snow in my skull
    when it caves in,
It could snow where my stomach
    my intestines were,
Inside my balls, inside
    where my cock was
It could snow, it could drift,
    white, deep,
It could cover my skeleton
    snowing inside where my body was
So many years.

Learning the Constellations

As there are constellations in the nightsky,
So there are constellations underground—
      for example, I hereby recognize
The constellation that exists
      if you connect with imaginary lines
All the undiscovered underground
      Tyrannosaurus skeletons.
And now I see and connect with imaginary lines
      into constellations
All the skeletons of all the dinosaurs that exist
      in the darkness underground.
And just as the stars send down their rays
      and each ray hits, enters, affects us,
So the dinosaur skeletons underground
      send up their rays and each ray
         hits, enters, affects us.
And to think the constellations in the nightsky
      are only 100,000 years old,
To think Tyrannosaurus had no Orion or Dipper
      to admire,
To think long before the constellations above we love
      came into being
And long after the constellations above we love
      have changed,
The skeletons underground remain.
Our skeletons gone, the great assembled dinosaur skeletons
      in our museums gone, America so far gone
         no one remembers what it was,
      and the nations that follow so far gone
         no one remembers what they were,
While the constellation of fossil Tyrannosaurs
      remains embedded in the nightsky
         of solid rock.

On Learning On the Clearest Night
Only 6000 Stars Are Visible
To the Naked Eye

If seeing only 6000 stars with naked eye
      awestrucks us to topple
            in drunken ecstasy
Or piss looking up in devout praise of being,
What would happen if we could truly perceive,
      comprehend and experience
         the zillions
    of stars galaxies universes
          pastpresentfuture?

And if, as scientists agree, we only use
      10% of our brain's potential,
Then the astonishment we sense
         is only 10% of the astonishment
    we could sense,
And so it would seem that what seems
      like dots of light twinkling
         in pretty patterns
    moving across the black
         is really enough to shatter us
    like goblets when the soprano
         hits the highest note.

And if the 10% of the brainpower we do use
      is ignorant of the 99.9% of the totality
         of the Universe,
    perhaps a li'l vino in our goblet
         ain't a bad idea—
Perhaps a flask of wine
      in deep wilderness night
         is more powerful
    than the largest telescope.

Star-Struck Utopias
of the 21st Century

What if Society became so obsessed with the stars
    as a result of Emerson's epiphany
"If the stars came out only one night in a thousand years
    how people would believe and adore
        and preserve from generation to generation
    remembrance of the miracle they'd been shown"
That everyone started sleeping during the day
    so they could stay up all night
        star-gazing, star-thinking, star-dreaming,
Being in the Milky Way so they could have
    maximum exposure to the Universe
        beyond Earth and our own Star.
Rather than being consumed by human history,
    art, literature, music, religion, politics, business,
        consumed by the stars,
    hunger to be with them and
        star-roving MilkyWaydom,
So much so that people spent more time
    looking at the Milky Way than at each other,
        more time looking up
    than straight ahead or down.
Total blackout in all cities—no streetlights, stoplights, carlights,
    driving at night illegal,
        no lights in buildings but candles,
Whole populations thronging to darkened
    stadiums and skyscrapertops
        to sit holding hands en masse
    and look up at the billion-year spree
        of the realm of the nebulae!

Milky Way Exposé from Gogebic Peak

Getting a poor sleep worrying if the sky will clear
    and unspeakably brilliant starry night come out
        and I'll miss it,
Whether I should open my sleepingbag
    and open the tent-window to see,
        and if it's clear
    get up, have a cup of coffee
        and stay up all night
    getting high with the stars.
Brandy and marijuana my telescope,
    collapsed on my back on
        amygdaloidal basalt Keweenawan lava-flow rock
    Kaug Wudju Paigwudawdizzid
        I starplunge into cosmos for hours
    as cool wind roars over me,
Or while bard owls hoot in the valley,
    parade back and forth on cliff-edge trail
        in intoxicated fervor
    (careful not to topple when I tipple)
        reunited with the energy and enthusiasm
    the high-spiritedness of my youth
        feeling I didn't let my boyhood down
    after all.
Glorious Milky Way travel till long after midnight
    exhaustion tents me.
Falling asleep thinking star massage,
    constellation acupuncture,
        remembering my youngman infatuation
    with getting high under nightsky
        celebrating the Milky Way
    till the birth of day,
Witnessing the starry universe Gogebic circles through,
    the vast forest twinkled over by stars,
        the night forest soothed, cooled,
    jeweled by stars—
The stars are shafts of light, erections of light
    lightyears long ejaculating across space and time
        fucking my eyes into my brain, or
The nightsky in reality a vagina
    or infinite vaginas side by side,
        each a sponge-tunnel with
    contoured plush niches
        of light and pleasure,
    textured labyrinths milking my brain—

the stars are vaginas of light,
each lightyear a vagina of light
Vaginas of light
millions of lightyears long
which my eyes penetrate—
My eyes fuck the nightsky
as much as the cocks of all time fucked
voluptuous vaginas.
Flat on my back Milky Way plunged,
no sense of the Earth under me,
swallowed into the infinite
Fathoming no more white dots on black background
but gaping depths deep into space
with endless fireballs
in tunnel'd chasms!
Realizing more stars behind every star I see
than all the stars in our galaxy!
Epiphanying wherever I look in the nightsky
I see stars!
Nightsky not black at all but white!
There's no black!
Just various shades of white
at various distances!
What seems black on closer scrutiny
reveals itself to be
white very far away!
Fallen asleep star-oggler,
Breathe free and easy in your downfilled bag
alone in the Wilderness
As the Earth Globe floats onward
with the other heavenly bodies
through Outer Space.

Subterranean Rivuletgurgle

Two-thirds the way to the summit
High above timberline on the switchback trail
Passing incredible jumbles of huge granite rocks,
Pausing, panting, to rest
    on a comfortable-looking
        lichen-covered stone,
Somewhere below where I sit
    a cheerful gurgling sound:
Rivulet, rivuletgurgle,
    subterranean rivuletgurgle.
Oh, I think, oh,
If only everyone could hear this,
    under all these rocks and boulders,
        chuckle, murmur,
    flowing, gushing,
In the dark underground,
While brooklets above sparkle in the sun
    edged by lush green grass
And yellow purple blue white red orange wildflowers
    with yellow purple blue white red orange butterflies
        slurping them.
No way to ever see you
    or drink from you
        (unless I return here with dynamite
    and blast my way to you)—
Only hear you for a few minutes
    before I rise and push on up
        to another monolithic mythic
    13,000 foot peak and 360-degree visionary vista
    I've never been.
Oh little gurgler below me, I suppose
    you've been gurgling here
        every hot afternoon
    the last million years.
I might've paused for a breather
    on a hundred other rocky vista spots
        on Mount Audubon's bouldery flank,
I might never've heard you
    and still been a devout lover of creeks
        and riversounds,
I might never've considered the reverberations
    of somewhere under boulders
        in the dark:
    darkrivuletgurgle,

darkrivuletgurgle...
But beyond words,
Beyond thoughts and dreams,
Beyond lyrics, elegiacs, rhapsodics,
  declarations, invocations, proclamations,
Before humans existed, before dinosaurs,
Ancient sounds: rain, thunder, wind, surf,
  lakelapping, waterfallroar and rivuletgurgle.
Subterranean rivuletgurgle—
Help us, heal us,
For you let gurgle a rivuletgurgle
  that could save the world.

Campfire Talk

Lonely, contemplating suicide?
Go alone into the forest, find a clearing,
Gather wood, build a fire, stay up all night
    with the fire and the stars.
Have a little blackberry brandy as your telescope
    to bring the stars closer in.
The sound of the fire, the smell of the fire,
The light and heat of the fire
    will help you, heal you.
A campfire's a Paleolithic experience
    we can all still have.

Renew the pledge of brotherhood round the fire.
Renew the pledge of sisterhood round the fire.
Hold hands in a circle and each make
    the sacred vow and pledge
And then silence, silence
    and the fire,
But really you're alone,
You only imagined your friends
    and lovers near,
Only imagined all the poets you love
    holding hands round the fire as one.

The flames recede,
The logs fall in among themselves,
Sparks fly up, a puff of smoke, a sigh,
    the fire dies down.
The cold creeps in and you draw nearer
    the ebbing flame,
And then the embers, the embers glowing
    softly red
While above the startling stars
    and forest smell rush in
    as eyes adjust to the dark.

The towering ancient trees nearby
Cease being lit
    by flickering light.
Warm your hands one last time
    over the dying fire.
Remain. Remain long
    after the fire is out,
Long after the cold creeps in.

Look up at the stars
     longer than you ever have
     and maybe ever will.

Renew the pledge of friendship round the fire.
Renew the pledge of love around the fire.
Make the vow of vows under the stars.
Renew, renew around the campfire
     in the wilderness under a wilderness of stars.
And then silence, silence and the expiring fire
     and the silent continuous movement
     of Stars and Earth in Space
Till the embers fade away—
     and with the first light of day
     shoulder your pack and head forth.

NOTES

Last Words

Wanbli Galeshka wana ni he o who e—Oglala Sioux for "The spotted hawk is coming to carry me away." One of the ghost dance songs.

"a perfect stranger by the name of Whitman"—Charles Whitman, University of Texas student who, from the 300-foot campus tower, shot and killed 14 and wounded 30 in 1966.

Factory

In the spring of 1970 I sold myself to Factory in order to make money to buy freedom to study and write Poetry. I enlisted at CCC—not Civilian Conservation Corps, but Continental Can Co., Plant 77, one of over 200 they operated at that time. Surrounded by barbed wire fence, along the Milwaukee River in Milwaukee, Wisconsin it was the largest can factory in the world under one roof. I worked in the press dept., packaging the tops and bottoms of cans into narrow bags or cardboard tubes as they came from a machine called a press which punched them from sheets of aluminum. The press machines were like huge machine-guns except rather than shooting bullets they shot lids: 1000 can lids a minute advancing toward me in a long cylindrical column down a long narrow chute. Once packaged, the lids were moved by fork-lift trucks called hysters to the other side of the dept., where they were run through machines called minsters. The sole purpose of the minsters, each of which cost half a million dollars, was to stamp fliptops onto the lids. The minsters were even louder than the presses. Each new worker had his ears measured and was given a set of earplugs in a tiny carrying case and was expected to wear them at all times on the job. They helped, but only somewhat. When you lay in bed waiting to fall asleep, the sound of the machines would still be ringing in your ears as loud as if two shells were put next to them and you were hearing the sea. Two months after I quit, the machines still ringing in my ears, I sat down with notes I'd jotted on the job and began arranging and expanding them into the 13 sections of "Factory."

Australopithecus—early human beings who lived three million years ago in Africa.

"Even the most ethereal vision of the mystic is knowledge much as an amoeba might be said to know a man."—line from Kenneth Rexroth's long poem "The Dragon and the Unicorn."

"Engulfed Cathedral"—a piano prelude by Debussy.

Martin Eden—great novel by Jack London I read when I was 16 and which inspired me to become a writer.

De mortuis nil nisi bonum—a Latin saying: "Speak nothing but good of the dead."

Baluchitherium—the Earth's largest land mammal, an 18-foot-tall hornless rhinoceros that lived in Asia 20 million years ago.

Chidiock Tychborn—a 1500s youth sentenced to beheading. The only poem we have by his name is the haunting lyric he wrote the night before he died: "Lines Writ By One in the Tower, Being Young and Condemned to Die." The refrain line is "And now I live, and now my life is done." Learned this poem (also the poems of Wilfred Owen) from James Wright during the summer of 1968.

Teratornis—an extinct carrion-eating cousin of the condor, with a wingspread of 12 feet, the largest flying bird in the history of life.

Ghost Dance—ritual dances and songs practiced by the Plains Indians in the 1880s, by whose repetition they believed they could magically make the white man vanish, the buffalo return, and all Indians live in peace on their ancestral lands.

Puberty of Smell
When a friend of mine returned from the Vietnam War, he went back to the factory he worked in before being drafted. After his first day back on the job, he locked himself in his bedroom. His mother knocked and asked if he wanted some dinner. There was no answer. Minutes later she heard the shot.

Rebecca Falls Epiphany
Rebecca Falls is a tumultuous waterfall in Quetico Provincial Park, a 1750-square-mile lake-forest-canoe wilderness in Ontario where I've spent more time alone than in my mother's womb and where this poem was written in early October 1974.

Alan Watts Dying in His Sleep Elegy
From his 1936 *The Spirit of Zen* through his *Beat Zen, Square Zen, and Zen* in the late '50s and until his death in 1973, Alan Watts' books did much to open the Western mind to Eastern modes of spirituality and other forms of "higher consciousness" (*The Joyous Cosmology*).

Childfoot Visitation
—occurred en route from San Francisco to Seattle to perform as the featured reader at a benefit poetry event for Amnesty International in 1982. Green Tortoise is a countercultural alternative to Greyhound: old hippie buses piloted by authentic colorful robust veterans of the '60s.

Lip-Licking Deer Shitting Meditation and Bedrock Mortar Full Moon Illumination

—were written in the fall of 1982 when I lived alone in a cabin built by Allen Ginsberg and Peter Orlovsky, which they named Bedrock Mortar (after the stone holes close to the cabin, as described in my poem), near Gary Snyder's homestead in the Sierra foothills.

Atheist Conches

Growing up I learned to pronounce "conch" with an "sh" ending, but later learned some people pronounce it with a hard "k" ending. That sounds too much like the word for when you hit your head on something—"conk." I still prefer "conch" to end with the sound of the sea—"shhhh"—and to reverberate with the word "consciousness."

Smuggling the Dust of Immortals

In July 1980 after spending 40 days and 40 nights alone in the Marble Mountain Wilderness in northern California, I returned to my apartment in San Francisco to discover I'd been invited to read at the Second International Festival of the Poet in Rome, Italy. Three days later, after my first jet ride in my life, I was there, where I read parts of "Factory." After the reading I spent a month in Europe. This poem happened on my return. The "antler'd dancer" is the renowned cave painting in southern France which appears in the finale of my long-poem "Factory."

Bubble-Boggled

When I read George Orwell's *1984* in highschool in 1964, I doubted I'd be alive when 1983 became 1984, but wondered where I'd be and what I'd be doing on New Year's Eve if I was. Rather than drunken noisy partying with friends, the solitude of the frozen Milwaukee river beckoned.

A decade after the poem was written, the 155-year-old North Avenue Dam to the south was removed; as a result, the flow of the river became narrower and faster so now it doesn't freeze safe enough to walk on in winter. Intrepid bubble-seekers, beware!

Ever since a child I have spelled the word "ogle" as "oggle" and pronounced it to rhyme with "boggle." After a 1990 reading in which I read "Bubble-Boggled," somebody informed me it should be pronounced to rhyme with "Gogol." When I wrote the poem I delighted in playing the short "o" sound in "oggle" off "boggle." I still prefer my dissident spelling and pronunciation. "Oggle" has more in common with "goggle" than "Gogol."

Unbrainwash Work-Ethic!

"We should do away with the absolutely specious notion that everybody has to earn a living. It is a fact today that one in ten thousand of us can make a technological breakthrough capable of supporting all the rest. The youth of today are absolutely right in recognizing this nonsense of earning a living. We keep inventing jobs because of this false idea that everybody has to be employed at some kind of drudgery because, according to Malthusian Darwinian theory, he must justify his right to exist. The true business of people should be to go back to school and think about whatever it was they were thinking about before somebody came along and told them they had to earn a living." —Buckminster Fuller

Me a Screaming Eco-Meemie?

Just back from the bluff overlooking Lake Michigan, at the corner of East Russell Avenue and South Superior Street in Milwaukee's Bay View area, is a historical marker at the site of the now long-gone Bay View Rolling Mills, a gigantic steel plant. On May 5, 1886, Wisconsin Militia fired into thousands of workers peacefully demonstrating there for an 8-hour workday. Seven people, including two boys, were killed. The Milwaukee killings occurred only one day after the Haymarket Riot in Chicago and these incidents helped to stifle, but ultimately to inspire, the establishment of the 8-hour workday.

Lucky Trees

Love of trees led me to fully explore and perceive the implications of trees as sexual beings and lovers. Example of trees which are separately male and female: Ginkgo, Aspen, Poplar, Willow, Ailanthus, Box Elder. Examples of trees that have male and female flowers on the same tree: Oak, Elm, Maple, Birch, Walnut, Sycamore. (I recited this poem in conjunction with the ceremonial tree planting during the dedication of the Allen Ginsberg Library building in Boulder on July 3, 1994.)

Everything Is Different Now

Robert A. Wallace, in his book *How They Do It*, relates: "In some species of octopuses, the copulatory arm of the male breaks away from his body and swims through the water as an 'independent' animal. These wandering arms somehow seek out females and enter their siphons, faithfully depositing sperm packets. Then the arms die, their corpses hanging from the female's body, producing the strange nine-armed octopuses which were the source of incessant speculation until the mating habits of octopuses were better known."

Boyhood Waterfall Offering

This poem explores one of the archetypal boyhood visionary experiences in the Wilderness, juxtaposing a boy's infinitesimal gift to the Infinite with the frothy gargantuan spume of a thundering waterfall. Any adventurous enough to try this, please be careful not to slip into the wat'ry cataclysm.

Hot Summer Night Rendezvous

In a small Northwoods drugstore, I discovered among the books on a solitary standing bookrack *Killer Clown*, the story of John Wayne Gacy who brutally tortured and killed 33 boys in Illinois. And I thought how any boy could buy this book about a man who killed boys, but no book there about a man who loved boys or about boys who loved each other. Now in the midst of the AIDS epidemic and in the wake of the Dahmer horrors, it seems more than ever time to recognize and respect the absolute naturalness of spontaneous occurrences of true-hearted same-sex affection.

Tell the Judge...Your Honor
and *Waterfallsexual*

Inspired by sensing the expansion of the Kinsey Continuum of sexual behavior (from exclusively heterosexual to exclusively homosexual with degrees of bisexuality in between) to include and be included by Nature. Whitman wrote about the nature-lover poet—"The Earth receives and returns his affection: he will stay with her as the bridegroom stays with the bride. The cool breath'd ground, the slumbering and liquid trees, the just-gone sunset, the vitreous pour of the full moon, the tender and growing night, he salutes and touches, and they touch him. The sea licks him all over with its tongues, the wind's soft tickling genitals brush against him, dazzling and tremendous the sunrise ravishes him."

Underwater Lake Michigan Socrates

Morgan Gibson—Midwest poet and scholar who has lived and taught in Japan since the late '70s. Founder of the UW-Milwaukee creative writing program, this pacifist was stripped of tenure, and his poet wife Barbara fired outright, for their participation in the May 1970 nationwide student strike in the wake of Nixon's invasion of Cambodia. See his *Among Buddhas in Japan*, *Revolutionary Rexroth*, *The Great Brook Book* and *Speaking of Light*. Gibson gave me the bust when I visited his summer cottage on Crystal Lake while in Frankfort, Michigan to give a reading on Thoreau's birthday.

Pussysmell Candlelight

The candle came into play during initial difficulty in attempting to activate the hetero side of my sexuality. This common "first time" problem, due to nervousness and unfamiliarity in exploring *terra incognita,* was duly transcended.

Pussy Feels Like

"Enlightenment is indescribable, but the closest thing to it is every pore of your body being a vagina." —Sri Ramakrishna

Anthem
—records my spontaneous response to unexpected playing of "The Star-Spangled Banner" at outdoor classical music concert in wake of Gulf War.

Sweet-Talk
Some critics said I'd written too many "outcries of outrage" and should "lighten up," so I wrote this. Sometimes charming helps when alarming.

Job Replacement for Loggers of Old-Growth
At the "EcoGlasnost" Conference (so dubbed by Allen Ginsberg) at Kerouac Poetics School in Boulder in July '90, we poets and ecologists who participated unanimously agreed there should be a moratorium on cutting any more ancient old-growth virgin climax forest, seeing as 95% had already been wiped out. Yet no one provided any suggestions as to how the loggers who'd lose their jobs would survive. So I wrote this poem for the loggers, trying to come up with non-ecocidal job ideas of beauty, meaning, imagination, ecstasy and fulfillment. Some might say my proposed jobs are preposterous. Yeah, but annihilating 95% of America's primeval forest isn't preposterous?

Proving What?
"A fool sees not the same tree that a wise man sees." —William Blake
"I got more from a tree than from any priest." —John Muir

Star-Struck Utopias of the 21st Century
For millennia those lost on land or sea looked up at the stars for direction, so the human species as a whole is lost on its own home planet, and in its own bodies and minds, and we need to recover our bearings by observing our position in the starry Cosmos. Wouldn't people be more cosmic if they spent more time under the nightsky engulfed in the Milky Way?

Milky Way Exposé from Gogebic Peak
Kaug Wudju Paigwudawdizzid means "Porcupine Mountain Hermit" in Ojibway. Gogebic means "Place of the Divine" in Ojibway.

Campfire Talk
John Muir declared that in Wilderness "lies the hope of the world." If that's true, and I have no doubt that it is, we need to preserve all the fast-vanishing wilderness that remains and get the one all-eclipsing, grossly overpopulous species back into a decent proportion to the rest of the spectrum of Life, and nurture the return of wilds and wildlife that have been rashly eradicated—and we need to immerse ourselves deeper and deeper in the wildest wilds. "Wilderness has answers to questions we don't even know how to ask yet."—Nancy Newhall.

ACKNOWLEDGMENTS

Periodicals:

A'ama Letters (Hawaii)
Abiko Quarterly (Japan)
Above the Bridge
Abraxas
Action
AIM Magazine
All Alone With Everything
Alemantschen—a Journal of Radical
Ecology (Switzerland) German translation
of   excerpts from "Factory"
Alley Cat Productions
Alpha Beat Soup
Ambrosia
American Poetry Review
American Writing
Am Here Forum
Amicus Journal
Androgyne
Angelflesh
Angelflesh Extra
Art Muscle
Arthur
Atom Mind
Avalanche
Babyfish
Bakunin
Ball Peen
Bathos Journal
Bay Windows
Beatlicks
Beatniks From Space
Beginner's Mind Broadside
Beloit Poetry Journal
Between the Species
Big Fireproof Box
Big Fish
Big Hammer
Big Head Press Broadside Series
Big Scream
Birthstone
Black Cross
Black River Review
Black Swan Review
Blank Gun Silencer
Blake Times

Blood and Guts (Lullabye Jesus)
Blow
Blueboy
Blueline
Blue Jacket (Japan)—Japanese translations
Bluff City
Bohemian (Japan)
Bombay Gin
Bouillabaisse
Brahma
Brass City
Breathe on the Living (LP sound recording)
Bugle American
BullHead #1 ("Save the Serpent Mound"
      issue)
Café Review
Calapooya Collage
Catalyst
Cedar Hill Review
Celebrate the Self
Cer*Ber*Us
Changing Men
Chelsea
Chiron Review
Christopher Street
CoEvolution Quarterly
Coffee Break Secrets
Cokefish
cold-drill
Confrontation
Connecticut Poetry Review
Contact II
Country Connections
Cover
Coyote's Dance
Crazy Shepherd
Cream City Review #1
Croton Bug
Crystal Drum
Current
Davka
Delirium
Denver Quarterly
Details
disturbed guillotine
Dockernet (Switzerland)

Dogfish Head Poetry Zine
Dream Machinery
Dream Network
Dreamworks
e-Amicus: Amicus Journal Internet Website
Earth First! Journal
EarthLight, a Journal of the Religious
    Society of Friends
EcoNews
Edge (Japan)
EIDOS
ELF: Eclectic Literary Forum
Experimental Audio Directions: Abscond
Express
Exquisite Corpse
Facet
Fahrenheit 451
Fearless
5 AM
Friction—special "Obscure Genius" issue
    ed. by Allen Ginsberg
Fuck!
Galley Sail Review
Ganymede
Garden of Delights
Gay Sunshine
Giants Play Well in the Drizzle...
Girder
Glyphs, a Journal of the Nevada City
    Literary Guild
God's Bar
Grasslands Review
Great Lakes Poetry Project , a Journal of
    the Marquette Poetry Society
Greenfield Review
Green Fuse
Green Mountains Review
Grist On Line
Groundwork
Gypsy
Haight Ashbury Literary Quarterly
Half Dozen of the Other
Hammers
Hanging Loose
Hart
Heaven Bone
"Hey, listen!"
High Country News
Hodge Podge Poetry
Holy Smoke Free Online Journal
Holy Titclamps

Home Planet News
House Organ
I AM
Images
Impetus
In Context, a Quarterly of Humane
    Sustainable Culture
Infinity Limited
Intuitive Explorations
Ironwood
James White Review
Japan Environmental Monitor (Japan)
Jemez Thunder
Journal of Progressive Human Services
Jump River Review
Just Write
Kaspahraster
Kenyon Review
Kink
Kumquat Meringue
Kootenay Split Shift Workbook
Kyoto Journal (Japan)
Kyoto Review (Japan)
Lactuca
Lame Duck
La Selva Subterranea
Letter eX
Lilliput Review
LINK
Lips
Lomakatsi
Longhouse
Long Shot
Lost, Beat & Broke in Milwaukee
Louder Than Bombs
Lucid Moon
Lynx Eye
Marquette Monthly
Maryland Poetry Review
Magical Blend
Michigan Voice
Mickle Street Review
Midwest Headwaters Earth First! News
Mildred
Milwaukee Area Greens
Milwaukee Journal
Milwaukee Magazine
Milwaukee Weekly
Minnesota Review
Mirage
Moongate de Homo Sentiens

Mothering
Nambla Journal
Napalm Health Spa
Nerve Cowboy
New Blood
New Uranian
New York Quarterly (including #52 containing a craft interview with Antler)
Nexus
Nightsun
Noctiluca
North Coast Review
North Country Anvil
O.ars
Olympia Review
One Voice, a Journal of Jeffersonian Democracy
Orphic Lute
Outpost Exchange
Oz Notes (Kansas City Area Pagan Newsletter)
Painted Bride Calendar
Paisley Moon
Pantheist Vision
Paramour
Parnassus Literary Quarterly
Passaic Review
Peaky Hide
Pebbles
Pemmican
Philae
Planet Detroit
Pleiades Magazine
pLopLop
Plumbers Ink
Poesflesh
Poetry Flash
Poetry International
Poetry Motel
Poets On: Offspring
POETS on the Line (on Internet)
Pome
Poetry San Francisco
Potpourri
Prairie Wind
Printed Matter (Japan)
Prophetic Voices
Pudding
Quarterly Newsletter of the Wisconsin Intellectual Freedom Coalition
Radio Free Marin

Rag Shock
Rain City Review
RaiZirr
Rattle
Riverrun
River Styx
Riverwest Review
RFD
Rocky Ledge
Sackbut Press Poemcard Series
San Francisco Sunday Examiner-Chronicle
Santa Fe Sun
Seems
Semiotext(e)
Sepia (England)
Shepherd Express
Shoes
Skidrow Penthouse
Skinner's Irregular Horse
Sing Heavenly Muse!
Small Pond
Smellfeast
Sonoma Mandala
Spaceball Ricochet
Spike
Split Shift
Starquest
Storm Warning!
Struggle
Sumari Bulletin
Sun-Optikos
Synaesthetic
Tabula Rasa
Talisman
Talking Leaves
Talking Raven Quarterly: Media Madness Issue
The Advocate
The American Voice
The Artful Mind
The Bellingham Review
The Body Politic
The Bridge
The Burning World
The Coffee Cup (Cosmic Café)
The Community Endeavor
The Dallas Review
The Endless Mountains Review
The Fifth Estate
The Gatekeeper
The Hollins Critic

The Holy Bi-Bull
The Holy Teenage Incest Chronicle Thing
the howling mantra
The Iconoclast
The Lucid Stone
The Muir View
The Needle's Eye
The New Censorship
The Northern Review
The Orator: Newsletter for the Milwaukee
    Chapter of NORML
The Peace Release (from Chicago's Peace
    Museum)
The Penis Mightier
The Plaza (Japan—Japanese translations)
The Plough: North Coast Review
The Quest
The Redneck Review: Iconoclasts Issue
The Rejection Notice
The Rocky Mountain Oyster
The Round Table
The Shepherd
The South End: Alternative Arts Issue
The Spectacle
The Star Beacon
The Sun
The Trumpeter: Journal of Ecosophy
    (British Columbia)
The Warrior Poet
The Wayne Literary Review
The World
Third Coast Archives
Third Rail
Tin Ear: Wire Mother
Total Abandon
Touchstone
Tonantzin
To Topio
Urbanus
Utne Reader
UWM Post
Vajradhatu Sun
Vice Versa
Vinyl Elephant
Voices
Wauwatosa News Times
Whole Earth Review
Wilderness
Wind
Windfall
Window Panes

Window Panes Be My Valentine
Windwatch (High Wind)
Wisconsin Academy Review
Wisconsin Light
Wisconsin Natural Resources
Wisconsin State Readers Association
    Journal
WisconsIn Step
Woodland Pattern Dial-a-Poem
Woodland Pattern Poem Flyer
Wordworks
XIB
Xtra! Church Wellesley Review (Toronto)
Zebra
Zeitgeist
Zen Tatoo
Zero
Zink
Zöne
ZZZ Zine

Anthologies:
A Day For a Lay: A Century of Gay Poetry,
    ed. Gavin Dillard, Barricade Books,
    New York, NY
American Poets Say Goodbye to the 20th
    Century, ed. Andrei Codrescu
    & Laura Rosenthal, Four Walls Eight
    Windows Press, New York, NY
An Ear to the Ground, ed. Marie Harris &
    Kathleen Aguero, University of
    Georgia Press, Athens, GA
Aqueous Reflections: A Terra Nova Book,
    ed. David Rothenberg & Marta
    Ulvaeus, MIT Press, Cambridge, MA
Asylums & Labyrinths, ed. Rob Cook,
    Rain Mountain Press, NJ
Atomic Ghost: Poets Respond to the
    Nuclear Age, ed. John Bradley,
    Coffee House Press, Minneapolis, MN
Between the Cracks: The Daedalus
    Anthology of Kinky Verse, ed. Gavin
    Dillard, Daedalus Press, San
    Francisco, CA
Boys of the Night, ed. John Patrick,
    STARbooks Press, Sarasota, FL
Brewing: 20 Milwaukee Poets,
    ed. Martin Jack Rosenblum,
    Giligia Press, New Hampshire
Celebrate America In Poetry & Art, ed.
    Nora Panzer, Hyperion Books for

Children of America with art from the
National Museum of American Art,
Smithsonian Institution, New York, NY

*Changer L'Amérique: Poésie Protestataire
des USA* (French translations), ed.
Eliot Katz & Christian Haye, La
Maison de la Poésie Rhône-Alpes
& Le Temps des CeRises Presses,
Paris, France

City Lights Journal #4, ed. Lawrence
Ferlinghetti & Nancy Peters,
City Lights Books, San Francisco, CA

City Lights Pocket Poets Anthology, ed.
Lawrence Ferlinghetti,
City Lights Books, San Francisco, CA,

City Lights Review, ed. Lawrence
Ferlinghetti & Nancy Peters, City
Lights Books, San Francisco,CA

Coffeehouse Poetry Anthology, ed, Larry
Smith & June King, Bottom Dog
Press, Huron, OH

Earth Prayers, ed. Elizabeth Roberts &
Elias Amadon, HarperSanFrancisco,
San Francisco, CA,

Erotic by Nature, ed. by David Steinberg,
Red Alder/Shakti Press, North San
Juan, CA

First Person Sexual, ed. Joani Blank, Down
There Press, San Francisco, CA

*Fresh Water: Poems from the Rivers, Lakes
and Streams*, ed. Jennifer Bosveld,
Pudding House Press, Johnston, OH

From the Tongue of the Crow, ed. Allyson
Bennett, Wisconsin Review Press,
Oshkosh, WI

Gateway, ed. Denise R. Rapp, Potpourri
Publications, Prairie Village, KS

*Gathering Place of the Waters: 30
Milwaukee Poets*, ed. by Bill
Lueders, Gathering Place
Productions, Milwaukee, WI

Gay & Lesbian Poetry in Our Time,
ed. Carl Morse & Joan Larkin,
St. Martin's Press, New York, NY

*Heartpieces: Wisconsin Poets Against
AIDS*, ed. Norman Richards, Namron
Press, Milwaukee, WI

Heatwave, ed. John Patrick, STARbooks
Press, Sarasota, FL

*Higher Learning: Reading & Writing About
College*, ed. Patti See & Bruce Taylor,

Prentice Hall, Upple Saddle River, NJ

*How We Live Now: Contemporary
Multicultural Literature*, ed. John
Repp, Bedford Books, NY

Inner Weavings, ed. Peter Whalen, Wildfire
Press, Milwaukee, WI

Looking for Your Name, ed. Paul Janeczko,
Orchard Books, NYC

*Media & Communication, Multisource
Anthology for Grades 7-9*, Prentice
Hall Canada Inc., Scarborough,
Ontario

*Men of Our Time: Male Poetry in
Contemporary America*, ed. Fred
Moramarco & Al Zolynas, University
of Georgia Press, Athens, GA

Nada Poems, ed. David Cope, Nada Press,
Grandville, MI

New Directions Anthology #37, ed. by
James Laughlin, New Directions, New
York, NY

New Directions Anthology #53, ed. James
Laughlin, New Directions, New York,
NY

*Out of This World: The Poetry Project at
St. Mark's Church in the Bowery*,
ed. Anne Waldman, Crown, NY

Paperwork, ed. Tom Wayman, Harbour
Publishing, Madeira Park, B.C.,
Canada

Pierced by a Ray of the Sun, ed. Ruth
Gordon, Harper Collins, New York,
NY

*Pig Iron #16: Labor & the Post-Industrial
Age*, ed. Jim Villani & Naton Leslie,
Pig Iron Press, Youngstown, OH

*Pig Iron #18: The Environment: Essence
and Issue*

Pig Iron #19: The American Dream

*Poems for the Nation: A Collection of
Contemporary Political Poems*, ed.
Allen Ginsberg, Eliot Katz & Andy
Clausen, Seven Stories Press, New
York, NY

*Poetry Comes Up Where It Can: Poems
from the Amicus Journal 1990-2000*,
ed. Brian Swann, University of Utah
Press & the Natural Resources
Defense Council, Salt Lake City, UT

Poetry for Peace, The Peace Museum,
Chicago, IL

Prayers to Protest: Poems that Center & Bless Us, ed. Jennifer Bosveld, Pudding House Press, Johnstown, OH

Prayers at 3 A.M.: Poems, Songs, Chants, and Prayers for the Middle of the Night, ed. Phil Cousineau, HarperSanFrancisco, CA

Pushcart Prize XVIII: Best of the Small Presses 1993, ed. Bill Henderson, Pushcart Press, Wainscott, NY

Reclaiming the Heartland: Lesbian and Gay Voices from the Midwest, ed. Karen Lee Osborne & William J. Spurlin Jr., University of Minnesota Press, Minneapolis, MN

Remains of the Wasteland, Red Hen Press

Scorched Hands, ed. Dave Church, Pariah Press, Providence, RI

Sometime the Cow Kick Your Head, ed. Robert Wallace, Bits Press, Cleveland, OH

Son of the Male Muse, ed. Ian Young, Crossing Press, Trumansburg, NY

Stubborn Light: The Best of The Sun's Second Decade, ed. Sy Safransky, The Sun Publishing Co, Chapel Hill, NC

The Flutes of Power: Poetics of the Wild, ed. Walt Franklin, Great Elm Press, Rexville, NY

The Heartlands Today, Volume 1, Views of the Midwest, Bottom Dog Press, ed. Larry Smith & Nancy Dunham, Huron, OH

The Heartlands Today, Volume 2, —A Cultural Quilt

The Heartlands Today, Volume 7, —The Urban Midwest

The Journey Home: the Literature of Wisconsin through Four Centuries, ed. Jim Stephens, North Country Press, Madison, WI

The Largeness the Small Is Capable Of, ed. Craig Hill, Score Press, Pullman, WA

The Maverick Poets, ed. Steve Kowit, Gorilla Press, Santee, CA

The Soul Unearthed: Celebrating Wildness & Personal Renewal through Nature, ed. Cass Adams, Tarcher, L.A., CA

The Unitarian Universalist Poets: A Contemporary American Survey, ed. Jennifer Bosveld, Pudding House Press, Johnstown, OH

This Book Has No Title, ed. by Kathleen Wiegner and Roger Mitchell, Third Coast Press, Milwaukee, WI

Thus Spake the Corpse: An Exquisite Corpse Reader 1988-1998, ed. Andrei Codrescu & Laura Rosenthal, Black Sparrow Press, Santa Barbara, CA

To Be a Man: In Search of the Deep Masculine, ed. Keith Thompson, Tarcher, L.A., CA

Verse & Universe: Poems About Science and Mathematics, ed. Kurt Brown, Milkweed Editions, Minneapolis, MN

Viet Nam Generation Big Book, ed. Kali Tal, Viet Nam Generation Press, Woodbridge, CT

What Book!?—Buddha Poems from Beat to Hiphop, ed. Gary Gach, Parallax Press, Berkeley, CA

Wild Song—Poems of the Natural World (a selection of poems that appeared in *Wilderness* magazine), ed. John Daniel, University of Georgia Press, Athens, GA

Will Work For Peace: New Political Poems, ed. Brett Axel, Zeropanik Press, Trenton, NJ

Wisconsin Poetry (anthology issue of *Transactions*), ed. Carl N. Haywood, Wisconsin Academy of Sciences, Arts & Letters Press, Eau Claire, WI

Wisconsin Poets' Calendar 1982, 1983, 1984, 1987, 1988, 1990, 1991, 1992, 1993, 1994, 1995, 1996, 1997, 1998, 2000, Wisconsin Fellowship of Poets

Working Classics, ed. Peter Oresick & Nicholas Coles, University of Illinois Press, IL

World's Edge, ed. Sherry Reniker, Word Press, Kawasaki, Japan

Books (poems quoted in books not anthologies):

A Life of Kenneth Rexroth, Linda Hamalian, Norton, New York, NY

An Invitation to Environmental Philosophy, Anthony Weston, Oxford University Press, Oxford, England

Back to Earth: Tomorrow's Environmentalism, Anthony Weston, Temple University Press, Philadelphia, PA

Bringing Heaven Down to Earth: A Practical Spirituality of Work, Eric S. Dale, Peter Lang Publishing, Inc., New York, NY

Dreaming the Lion: Reflections on Hunting, Fishing and a Search for the Wild, Thomas McIntyre, Countrysport Press, Traverse City, MI

Hunting the Snark, Robert Peters, Asylum Arts Books, NM

Poet-Chief: The Native American Poetics of Walt Whitman & Pablo Neruda, James Nolan, University of New Mexico Press, Albuquerque, NM

Practicing Desire: Homosexual Sex in the Era of AIDS, Gary W. Dowsett, Stanford University Press, Stanford, CA

Simple in Means, Rich in Ends: Practicing Deep Ecology, Bill Devall, Peregrine Smith Books, Salt Lake City, UT

The Art of Pilgrimage: The Seeker's Guide To Making Travel Sacred, Phil Cousineau, Conari Press, Berkeley, CA

Chapbooks:

A Second Before It Bursts, Woodland Pattern Books, Anne Kingsbury & Karl Gartung, Milwaukee, WI, 1994

Ever-Expanding Wilderness (chapbook by that title was part of deluxe artbook issue #2 of *Stiletto* subtitled "The Disinherited") Howling Dog Press, Michael Annis, Denver, 1992

Learning the Constellations, Backwoods Broadsides Chaplet #52, Sylvester Pollet, Ellsworth, ME, 2000

Subterranean Rivulet, Falling Tree Press, Howard Nelson, Moravia, NY, 1996

Your Great-Great-Grandfather's Puberty Boners, Permeable Press, Brian Clark San Francisco, 1995

Awards:

Antler received the 1985 Whitman Prize of the Walt Whitman Association, which maintains Whitman's final home in Camden, NJ. In announcing the award, given to the author "whose contribution best reveals the continuing presence of Walt Whitman in American poetry," Whitman Association spokesperson Jean Pearson wrote of Antler: "His poems make audible the words of the earth, with original energy, insouciance and affectionate comradeliness toward all beings."

Publication of *Last Words* in 1986 caused Antler to be awarded the 1987 Witter Bynner Prize from the American Academy & Institute of Arts & Letters in New York City.

"Your Poetry's No Good Because It Tries to Convey a Message" won the Madeline Sadin Award from *New York Quarterly*.

"Hot Summer Night Rendezvous" won first place in the Wisconsin Poets Respond to AIDS Contest in 1990.

"Somewhere Along the Line" won a Pushcart Prize in 1993.

Also:

"Bringing Zeus To His Knees" appeared in the *Shadowgraph Project*, a traveling poetry/art exhibit curated by Karl Young, 1990.

"Your Poetry's No Good Because It's Too Easy to Understand" was included in "A Piece of Peace: Poetry for the Walls," a poetry/art exhibit at Chicago's Peace Museum, Fall 1994.

"Lip-Licking Deer Shitting Meditation" was published in *Woodland Pattern Poemcard Series* in English and in Chinese translation by Yuan Yuan (in conjunction with Antler's reading with poets from China at Museum of Modern Art in NYC and Woodland Pattern in Milwaukee in 1988).

"Eye to Eye" is on a plaque in the Midwest Express Convention Center in downtown Milwaukee—one of the writings by Wisconsin authors selected to be put on permanent display via the Public Arts Project.

"Draft Dodgers vs. Poetry Dodgers" was made into a poster by University of Idaho-Boise's Ahsahta Press for their poetry in public places project and also appears on the west wall of the middle room in Woodland Pattern Literary Center in Milwaukee.

"Now You Know" was set to music for voice and piano by Pulitzer Prize-winning classical music composer David Del Tredici.

Words from "Bedrock Mortar" were set amid a woodcut illustration of the poem by artist Letterio Calapai.

The author also wishes to thank:

The Milwaukee Artists Foundation, the Cream City Foundation, Arts Futures, the Wisconsin Arts Board, PEN American Center, James Ingram Merrill, Omega Institute, the Jack Kerouac School of Disembodied Poetics, the Culture & Animals Foundation, the Northwoods Wilderness Recovery Project, Woodland Pattern and the Lila Wallace-Reader's Digest Fund for grants and special teaching/performance opportunities that helped give me time to work on, finish and share the poems in this book.

Special Thanks:

To Allen Ginsberg in Eternity for his friendship and encouragement from 1976 to 1997 and the ongoing consolation and inspiration of his spirit,

To Jeff Poniewaz for blessing me with his Whitmanic cameradohood since 1966 and his invaluable "sounding board" revision assistance to me over all those years,

To Kara Moore for teaching me the other side of love,

To Lawrence Ferlinghetti for publishing *Factory* in 1980 as a book to itself in the City Lights Pocket Poets Series (#38),

To Robert Wyatt for publishing my *Last Words* book at long last in 1986 via his Available Press subsidiary of Ballantine Books.

To my Mother for giving birth to me and nurturing my poet spirit,

And to Walt Whitman, my spiritual father, for considering long and seriously of me before I was born.

ANTLER

Left to Right: Jeff Poniewaz, Antler, and Allen Ginsberg in Allen's Boulder apartment, 7-10-94. Photo by Steve Miles

Antler is the author of three books of poetry: the long-poem *Factory* and the collections *Last Words* and the forthcoming *Ever-Expanding Wilderness*. Antler was given the 1985 Walt Whitman Prize awarded to the author "whose contribution best reveals the continuing presence of Walt Whitman in American poetry." The appearance of *Last Words* in 1986 won Antler the 1987 Witter Bynner Award of the American Academy and Institute of Arts and Letters. He was celebrated by Allen Ginsberg, who called *Factory* a "definitely powerful epic by one of Whitman's 'poets and orators to come.'. . . the most enlightening and magnanimous American poem I've seen by anyone of '60s & '70s decades." When not wildernessing or travelling to perform his poems, Antler lives in Milwaukee, Wisconsin.